Science, freedom, beauty, adventure: What more could you ask of life? Aviation combined all the elements I loved.

Charles Lindbergh, the Spirit of St Louis. 1963

*To the pilots of all the worlds airlines,
past and present.*

ACKNOWLEDGMENTS

I want to thank my fellow crew- members, Captain Jack Keyes, Captain Rick Gordon and Flight attendant Kenda Browne, who have allowed me to use their names and tell their stories.

A special thanks to my Sister in Law and editor, Marilyn Ippolito who in an earlier life wrote letters of apology to the angry customers of America West Airlines. Her knowledge of the airline industry was of immeasurable help in pointing out flaws in my inadequate prose.

To Captain Jack Blaz, my friends Jack and Joan Kickham and Selwyn Hayward, thank you for reading my early manuscripts and steering me on a path to a better book.

William L. Ippolito
Dallas, Texas

Chapters

INTRODUCTION

The aviation industry celebrated an anniversary in 2002. Seventy-five years ago, on May 21, 1927, Charles A. Lindbergh, in his steel tube and fabric aircraft, the *Spirit of St. Louis*, departed Roosevelt Field, an airport just outside New York City. Piloting his small craft alone, Lindbergh navigated the 3,610 miles to Paris, France, in 33 hours and 30 minutes and arrived a hero. His daring and brave flight made him the world's first media celebrity. The real significance of his bold feat, however, was to show the practicality of the airplane as transportation. I like to think of Lindbergh as the father of the air transport industry.

The world had to suffer the great depression and World War II before flying in airplanes as ordinary transportation grew to be commonplace. Even then, it existed only for the very wealthy. In February 1946, TWA became the first U.S. airline to launch service to Europe flying a graceful four engine Lockheed Constellation named the *Star of Paris*. With re-fueling stops in Gander, Newfoundland and Shannon, Ireland, the flight from New York to Paris took nearly 20 hours, cutting half a day off Lindbergh's time. The round trip fare of $675 represented 27 percent of the average American's annual income of $2,500 in 1946. Air transportation for the masses would have to wait.

On October 26, 1958, Captain Samuel Miller guided the clipper *America*, his new Pan American World Airways Boeing 707 jet transport, from New York to Paris, inaugurating the first U.S. scheduled trans-Atlantic jet passenger service. The flying time was just under 8 hours. Overnight, flying time across the Atlantic was cut in half. In a mere 31 years and five months, the time to cross the Atlantic had shrunk from 5 days to 8 hours. In little more time than it takes to raise today's child to adulthood, send him or her to college and out on their own, the time to reach anyplace on earth diminished to a fraction of its previous amount. The credit belongs to jet transport aircraft. I call it the "Jet Age," and I was there at the beginning.

Jet aircraft democratized air travel. No longer is it the habitat of the privileged few. The 1946 round trip New York to Paris fare of $675 is equal to over $6000 in today's dollars. In the year 2002, one can purchase an off-season, round trip, New York to Paris ticket for hundreds less than the fare in 1946. Every day some 25 wide body aircraft, each capable of carrying at least 250 passengers, depart JFK International Airport for Paris, France. Wouldn't Lindbergh be delighted at what he wrought?

This book is about my life in the jet age, but even more it is the amazing story of the airline industry during that time. At the beginning of my airline career my company had 9,000 employees and 920 pilots. When I retired the count was 90,000 employees and 9,000 pilots. The growth in our industry matched the speed of its planes. This incredible growth, however, was not without pain and I have not left out the bad for only the good.

In the year 2003 we will celebrate the 100th anniversary of powered flight. During the ensuing years countless aviators, as skilled in the use of words as in the controls of flight, have put word to paper describing the esthetic experience of flight, to the delight of the uninitiated. I make no such pretensions. My story is about the airline cockpit and the long aluminum tube that follows it in innocence. The first true airliner I flew sat 28 passengers, two pilots and one stewardess and the last, 302 passengers, 3 pilots and 10 flight attendants. On that first aircraft, a DC-3, we worried about engine failure and in-flight fire, thunderstorms and fog; on the last, the Lockheed TriStar, our concerns had become terrorists, hi-jackings and air rage. This natural evolution from the mechanics of flying to the humanity of flight is as it should be. The fact that air transportation has arrived at this point is the reason why it is taken for granted by those who have little knowledge of its past. We have come from "will we get there?" to "will we be on time?" I am sure it is exactly what men like Lindbergh had in mind.

All of the stories written here are true and all of the people are real. The flight that serves as the framework of this tale is one I actually operated as pilot in command. The crew, however, has been taken from similar flights because they are some of my favorites and more representative of all airline crews.

You will notice that I often refer to my airline, Delta Air Lines, as my company. I mean this in a literal sense. Not the company I work for, but my company. I know of no other industry where greater loyalty exists among its employees. Perhaps it is because almost every employee of an airline interacts with the customer. There are few airline employees who do not suffer the wrath of a dissatisfied customer or cherish the delight of the customer who is happy. In no other industry that I can think of are the employees so intimately involved with those who use our product. In the past, there have been airline managers who forgot this. Most of their companies no longer exist.

Come fly with me (with apologies to the late Mr. Sinatra) as I take you from the dawn of the "Jet Age" and the evolution of the "Jet Set" to the present. No songwriter ever drew romantic inspiration from a propeller driven aircraft. John Denver however had no trouble being inspired by modern day air transport when he wrote "Leaving On A Jet Plane."

PROLOGUE
FEBRUARY 1994

"Because I am incorrigibly, now, a wanderer"---

-Beryl Markham, West Into The Night, 1942

The winter sun burns low on the western horizon, its brilliance filtered and diminished by the leaden marine air. Still, I find it necessary to install the tinted, removable sunshield above the cockpit instrument panel to further reduce the distracting glare. Now I can clearly see the flight instruments directly in front of me. There are three power levers on the Lockheed TriStar and they are tucked neatly in the palm of my hand. Using the thumb and little finger of my right hand, I crush the three levers together while using the palm of my hand to push the levers smoothly forward. With the ball of each foot pressed against the rudder pedals, I do a little squirm in my seat, not out of nervousness but as a way to lock myself in position so as to be at one with the controls. Three Rolls Royce turbofan engines begin their acceleration from idle, first with a low, mournful moan, then with increasing frequency, pitch, and volume... an ear splitting symphonic glissando, rising until the higher frequencies are above human comprehension.

The aircraft begins to move from its resting place at the takeoff end of runway 25-right. My eyes momentarily glance left, and I see the old Mines Field Air Terminal, built in the Spanish hacienda architecture of the 1930s. It is the original Los Angeles

5

International Airport, LAX to the travel industry, but now a preserved historic building. For a moment I can visualize an ancient DC-3 squatting in front of the old terminal anticipating the boarding of a few motion picture luminaries or corporate titans. There would be no crowded terminal, no long ticket counter lines, as few could afford the luxury of air travel in the 1930's. In any case, the Douglas Commercial Model 3 could only accommodate 21 passengers, one stewardess, and two pilots. I force my eyes back to the runway in front of me. This is not the time for nostalgic mental wanderings. I lock my gaze on the runway centerline. The far end is more than two-and-a-half miles away and I cannot see it because there is a slight rise halfway down that obscures the far end and makes the runway appear only half as long as it actually is. The greatest danger now is loss of engine power and I concentrate on keeping the nose-wheel on the painted white stripe marking the center of the runway, as any un-commanded deviation from the centerline could indicate an engine failure.

The raised runway centerline lights create a small rumble and I add a little pressure to the left rudder bringing the lights between the duel nose wheels. Perfect! The rumble ceases as our airspeed increases. If an engine fails before we reach V1, the takeoff decision speed, (about 130 knots) I will abort the takeoff. I have been assured by the second officer, backed by a mound of charts, graphs and manuals, that below this speed there is sufficient runway to come safely to a stop. On the other hand, if an engine fails after V1, these same charts, graphs and manuals have promised me the aircraft can continue its takeoff and climb safely to 1,000 feet above the ground where we can then execute all the proper procedures to safely return to earth. For myself, this has redefined the meaning of faith.

At 100 knots, our aircraft begins its protest. It is not designed for freeway cruising, and every little rut, groove or undulation in the runway is transmitted from the nose-wheel to my seat cushion and up my spine, through my body and out my arms until I must loosen my grip on the throttles or risk accidentally pulling them back, thus reducing the very power we must have to make truth out of the charts, graphs and manuals that promise so much.

In the cabin, the passengers are tense, watching the plastic overhead panels vibrate and shake, perhaps even prepared to duck if the overhead bins should open, and spill their lethal content.

As we pass V1, I remove my hands from the throttles, and begin a smooth pull on the control wheel, bringing the nose up to about 12 degrees above the horizon. As flight begins, there are additional mechanical protests as the landing-gear struts, unwilling to release their earthly grip, extend to support thousands of pounds of wheels and brakes. I call out "gear up" and, at last, the vibration and noise of our earth-bound machine dissolves into the smoothness of flight. It is no surprise to me that occasionally passengers applaud at this point. I am often of a mind to join them.

Our destination is Frankfurt, Germany —5,481 nautical miles from Los Angeles. In the cockpit with me are Rick Gordon, the first officer and Jack Keyes, the second officer. Ten flight attendants, all female, are in the cabin. On the day of this flight, February 12, 1994, it's rare to have a female cockpit crewmember, but equally rare to find an all-female cabin crew.

As the aircraft accelerates, I see Gordon's hand move toward the flap lever. He knows what is coming next, and doesn't need to be told what to do. However, procedure demands that I command flap retraction and I do so. Engine power is reduced for climb, and now we are aerodynamically at our best. There is a noticeable relaxation of tension in the cockpit, as we all understand that any abnormality that might occur at this point can be dealt with in a relaxed but precise manner. Still, there is little conversation between us other than those words necessary for the safe operation of our aircraft. I glance down at the departure chart that resides in a four-inch-thick leather-bound ring binder, just left of my seat. It is spotted with dried coffee stains—a reminder of a past indiscretion when I used it as a tray table. I confirm that I am following the mandatory departure procedure that requires us to make a climbing left turn to cross over Los Angeles Airport at 10,000 feet or above. It is not an easy task, as we are carrying 210,000 pounds of fuel and more than 200 passengers and crew. Though I know it is sheer silliness, I find myself using body English and a very un-technical "C'mon baby" to help our cause. Perhaps it helped. We cross the Los Angeles navigation fix with 50 feet to spare. Now we are pointed toward our destination, and I lower the nose allowing our aircraft to accelerate to 320 knots.

The air is smooth and our passengers are hungry. An instant after I turn off the "fasten seat belt" sign, I can hear the spring-loaded flight-attendant jump seat bang itself into the stowed position. They know, more than I do, that passenger expectations are high and it is time to go to work.

Jack Keyes, the second officer, calls out to me, "Can I get you something to drink, Captain?" It is strange to hear the word "captain" come from his lips because Keyes, at 73, is fifteen years older than I am, and thirteen years retired as a line captain on the Boeing 707. It is a federal mandate that no person shall serve as pilot on a commercial aircraft past midnight on the day before his 60th birthday. Jack, however, couldn't stay away from the industry he loved, and chose to take a subordinate position as second officer, or more accurately flight engineer, rather than retire. I am pleased with his choice. His experience can do no harm. As he leaves the cockpit headed for the galley, I am ashamed to realize he is more fit than I.

It is time now for me to speak to the passengers, for soon they will be distracted with movies and other in-flight attempts to quell anxieties and relieve boredom. With the aircraft being steered by autopilot, I reach for the public-address microphone. A glance at Rick Gordon is all that is needed to place the operation of the aircraft in his hands.

As I speak to the passengers in the most confident voice I can muster, I feel not one ounce of guilt that I am telling them lies. I tell them the flight will be smooth but I know no such thing. I tell them we will be there in 10 hours and 39 minutes ... perhaps. I tell them the weather is excellent when I know it is not. I know that telling them anything but good news will only increase their anxiety, and generate questions I cannot answer. What I do know is that we will get there within a reasonable time of our scheduled arrival. We will do our best to avoid clear-air turbulence, although there is no reliable way to do so. As for the weather, well it really doesn't matter, as far as we are concerned, as our aircraft and crew is capable of almost zero-visibility landings. In 10 hours and 39 minutes the earth will have rotated almost one-half its circumference, and the weather will not be what it was. And in fact, all of my lies may become truths.

Keyes returns to the cockpit empty-handed. The flight attendant has in good nature run him out of her galley. Her name is Kenda Browne, and she will bring us liquids. Kenda, part of the crew on my first line flight in 1963, will, in all likelihood, be part of a crew after I retire. She knows her job, and I am confident that only the direst circumstance would persuade her to seek help from one of the cockpit crew. It is to her and nine colleagues that our passengers will air their compliments and complaints. They are the frontline, and must sometimes bear the brunt of abuse and incivility, when all is not sweetness and contentment.

After Kenda delivers our beverages, she lingers for just a moment and reminds me of that first flight so many years ago. "Just look at you –the baby DC-6 flight engineer– all grown up and captain of his own big airplane." I do not know whether to blush, laugh or throw her out of the cockpit, and so I do all three ... but she is gone before I can complete my triple act.

As we cross Twenty-Nine Palms navigation fix, I glance down at our flight plan and note that next to the cryptic "TNP" is the number 1012. Ten hours and 12 minutes of flight time remaining to our destination. We have been aloft 27 minutes, and have arrived at our cruising altitude of 33,000 feet at precisely the minute, using precisely the fuel predicted by a dispatcher using a bank of computers 3,000 miles away. I am in awe of such precision. I glance down at the flight plan to see what artist created this masterpiece. It is DIBENEDETTO, spelled in all capital letters. I stifle a chuckle as my memory races back to a time when almost no one on this airline had a name that ended in "o." Below his name is our airline identification and flight number, DL 58, the international identification for Delta Airlines Inc. flight number 58.

The landscape slipping quietly beneath our cockpit segues from stark Southwestern desert and mountains to flat central plains with their neatly ordered section lines precisely oriented to true north. It is winter and the colors are overwhelmingly brown. The idle small talk among us has begun to wind down. Gordon busily surveys his navigation log. Keyes consumes lead in his automatic pencil at an alarming rate as he logs fuel burn and engine readings. My eyes do a quick sweep of the cockpit. Switches, dials and gauges are everywhere. I am incredulous that mere humans can work such complexity. All is well, as it usually is, lending truth to the old saw that, "Flying is hours and hours of boredom, punctuated by moments of stark terror."

As my eyes scour the sky ahead and the earth below, it is impossible to keep my mind from wandering back in time. Back to the summer of 1958, and my first job on an airplane. I was not the pilot, nor even a passenger. I was the piano player.

1958

"When starting an aviation career it is not unusual to be overwhelmed, terrified, suffer from lack of confidence and be just plain scared. As experience grows, self confidence replaces fear...But after a time, when you think you have seen it all, you realize your initial reactions to flying were correct." Author unknown.

Like an ancient pelican past its prime, the war-weary DC-4 lifts itself from the runway of Burbank Air Terminal, and heads north to Las Vegas. On board the aging four-engine propeller driven transport are 85 party-ready passengers who, having laid out $25 each, are entitled to round-trip air transportation, a bottle of champagne, one free dinner and a five-dollar Hacienda Hotel Casino chip. I am strapped to my seat, or rather to my piano bench. It is not my job to see them to their destination safely. Others on board are trained to do that. Instead, it is my job to make sure they arrive in a festive and free-spending mood. It is also my job to keep them distracted, to help them ignore the noise of the engines, the inevitable desert turbulence, and the lack of air-conditioning and pressurization. I am expected to do all this though I am not yet 21 years old, and have been aloft only once before for a brief ten-minute flight in a small plane.

I have come to this position as a music student at a local college. Performing in local bars and nightclubs is how I earn my living. The regular piano man for this flight, Charley Ray, a local Southern California musician of some repute asked me to

11

substitute on this evening. I am elated, frightened, nervous and grateful for the opportunity to go aloft. That I must play the piano and entertain does not enter my mind.

As the ancient pelican folds its wheels, I launch into a rousing rendition of "Won't You Come Home Bill Bailey?" Eighty-five festive voices, most as bad as mine, join with me. Ten hours later, on the return flight at four o'clock in the morning, not a peep will be heard.

I sit in the cockpit on the return flight, between the pilots and just behind the center control console where engine throttle, propeller controls and radios are arranged in a complicated array of confusion and mystery. I am mesmerized and completely infatuated with the magic of aviation. The two pilots chat amiably, and include me in their conversation. I am in awe that they find me worthy of notice.

As we approach Burbank Air Terminal the conversation between Mike the captain and Willie the co-pilot becomes more business-like and the reality of my presence is ignored as they go about their duties. There is a noticeable increase in tension as a weather report is received indicating deteriorating conditions at the Burbank airport. Mike snaps at Willie, "ask them to repeat that report, for Christ Sakes it was clear an hour ago." Willie obliges but the weather report remains unchanged. I become mildly alarmed while not sure even if I should be. As an innocent in the world of aviation, I know not if this is normal procedure or a crisis in progress. Mike banks the weary Douglas airliner sharply to the right and demands of Willie, "Do you see it?"
"Yes, just barely," Willie replies. I look where Willie is looking and see nothing resembling an airport. "O.K. I got it," Mike shouts as he banks our aircraft even more steeply to line up with the runway. Only then, just moments before touchdown, do I see the parallel line of runway lights through the murk and fog enveloping the city of Burbank and its airport. I am enthralled by the skill and daring shown by the two heroic airmen.

As a child during World War II, I was convinced that pilots were above mere mortals. Having watched John Wayne, Clark Gable and Van Johnson win the war against fascist and imperial tyranny, I became convinced that airplane pilots were more than ordinary men. The easy relaxed manner of my two new heroes, as they explained what they were doing, caused me to completely re-evaluate my own abilities and intelligence. They were much like me, and I could hardly believe it.

In my youth, I thought of aviation as mostly a military endeavor. At the end of WWII, trains were still the primary means of long-distance travel. The country's great airlines — United, American, TWA and Pan Am — spent the duration of the war carrying military personnel to and from wherever they were needed. Few civilians flew for personal reasons. After the war, civil aviation grew slowly. The occupation of airline pilot hardly existed. Growing up I had wanted to be an airplane pilot, but the concept of airline pilot did not occur to me until I saw John Wayne and Robert Stack in the motion picture *The High and The Mighty*.

No single event galvanized my passion for airline flying more than watching Wayne and Stack guide the stricken transport between the coastal hills southwest of San Francisco, to a safe landing. The 1955 movie, adapted from Earnest K. Gann's book of the same name, was a dramatic tale of a flight from Honolulu to San Francisco. With several Motion Picture Academy nominations, it won an Oscar for best film score. Of course I think it should have won best picture, best actor, best popcorn-eating movie, and every other conceivable award. I just could not get enough of this movie. It changed my life. I wanted to be an airline pilot but I had no idea how to go about it, and worse, what few talents I had in school (mostly musical) did not seem to lend themselves to flying airplanes. After all, everyone knows you have to be good at math, right? I had serious doubts about my ability to get past my fingers and toes. Everyone told me most pilots were standout athletes. I was a third-string high school football player.

13

And of course you must have the eyes of an eagle. I had no idea what my vision was, and I was too afraid to ask. So I went to college as a music major, and the dream lay dormant, pushed back in my mind, buried under the reality of my academic and physical shortcomings — that is, until the return flight from Las Vegas, sitting between Mike and Willie in the cockpit of their wheezy old DC-4, watching two ordinary men practice their extraordinary profession.

FLIGHT 58, TIME REMAINING 8:30

"Learn from the mistakes of others. You won't live long enough to make all of them yourself." Author unknown.

As we approach Salina, Kansas, the sky ahead dissolves into a deep royal blue. I turn around in my seat to the left, and press my nose to the cockpit side window. I can see only the very tip of the magnificent wing that allows us to remain aloft. Only a smaller nose would allow me to see more, yet, I do not need to see it, I know it is there: it is the last rays of the sun I seek. I am fascinated by the physical laws that will allow the sun and our aircraft to travel in opposite directions, only to meet again in a few hours face to face. Ahead of us is the blackness of the sub-arctic night. Soon there will be nothing to see below us, only the emptiness of the frigid Arctic Ocean.

It is quiet in the cockpit. Cruising flight in domestic airspace requires little more than the monitoring of instruments, and the occasional radio transmission to air traffic control, which observes our every movement on radar. I am not lulled into complacency however, as I know all too well it is at this point in the flight that passenger troubles often begin to emerge. The sharing of these adventures during quiet times serves to reduce the monotony of cruising flight and, not inconsequentially, experience is gained in how to safely resolve onboard disagreeableness. I laugh to myself as I recall a humorous incident in 1978 while in command of a Boeing 727 en route to Denver, Colorado.

15

***

I am humming "Oh, What A Beautiful Morning" quietly to myself, with my head turned to the left, looking out the cockpit window so the first officer cannot hear. The sky is blue, the morning air quiet. Life is good.

BANG! CRUNCH! A flight attendant has entered the cockpit, slamming the door behind her and crashing on the jump seat behind me. I am incredulous that 110 pounds can make so much noise. I turn around and see the tears that are about to rain on my parade.

"Are you OK?" I ask, knowing full well she is not.

"God, I hate kids," she bawls. "They're having a food fight, and I am not going back."

"Oh my," I said. Though a much stronger reaction was on the tip of my tongue, I held it in check. "Perhaps I better go back there and straighten things out."

I remembered we had boarded 40 pre-adolescents in Dallas, bound for a summer camp near Denver. While several adults had seen to their boarding, and more were to meet them in Denver, there was no adult accompanying them. Apparently my company felt that four flight attendants were more than enough to handle 40 rowdy kids and the 30 or so other paying passengers on our B-727. It was Saturday. Our four flight attendants were fairly new. None were old enough to be any of our passengers' mothers.

As I slowly got out of my seat, the first officer put on his oxygen mask, a procedure required when only one pilot is at the controls. I knew I had to do something that would make a strong impression on the little rascals, so I put on my coat and hat and tried to make myself look like some Third World military dictator.

16

Slipping into the serenity of first class, I could sense the chaos occurring just behind the curtain separating it from the rear cabin.

Throwing aside the curtain, I stomped into the maelstrom of economy class. I stood before them, feet apart, balled fists on my hips and a scowl on my face. The sight of an authority figure, behatted with lightning bolts, multiple stripes on my sleeves and adornments on my chest had a startling effect. The noise stopped. It got so quiet you could hear the sound of a banana cream pie sliding down the cabin wall. Then plop! It landed right at the foot of a pre-adolescent male armed with a creamy chocolate cake he'd prepped to launch across the cabin against his well-armed adversary five rows away. The debris of battle hung dripping from the seats. Turkey sandwich-shrapnel littered the floor. A few deadly chocolate chip cookies had left their mark on the cabin ceiling after ricocheting off the head of a hapless enemy. Pulverized potato chips were ground into the carpet by the advancing army.

"YOU HAVE FIVE MINUTES TO CLEAN UP THIS MESS," I roared in the most commanding voice I could muster. "OR I WILL TURN THIS PLANE AROUND, RETURN TO DALLAS, AND YOU WILL ALL BE ARRESTED."

I left the economy cabin as commandingly as I arrived. But passing through first class, I couldn't ignore the adult laughter and I broke up. In answer to one gentleman who jovially said, "You tell 'm Captain," I said: "That'll hold the little bas…err.. Rascals!"

The flight attendants passed out wet towels, walls were scrubbed, floors swept up as best they could, and silence was the tone for the duration of the flight. I sensed that they were not sure if they were going to camp, or to jail.

The camp director met the flight in Denver, and our formerly tearful flight attendant explained all that had passed.

17

Several months later I received from our public relations department a stack of apologetic letters written by each one of our pubescent perpetrators. I laughed long and hard as I read each very sincere apology probably done under the coercion of the Camp Director. Each letter, individually written, contained a common theme to all of them, best expressed by the one that started out like this.

"Dear Captain Bill: We are sorry we messed up your plane. I DIDN'T DO IT BUT I KNOW WHO DID."

FLIGHT 58, TIME REMAINING 7:21

"You start with a bag full of luck and an empty bag of experience. The trick is to fill the bag of experience before you empty the bag of luck." Author unknown.

Approaching the United States/Canadian border, Cleveland air traffic control center asks that we contact Toronto center. This is the logical progression of our flight. If we wish to fly in Canadian air space, then we must talk to Canadians. The first time I entered Canadian airspace, in 1978, I was stunned by how American they sounded (which of course they are!). I mean to say, they sound more American than U.S. Americans. In fact, when I travel around the USA as an airline pilot, what I don't hear is a standard American accent. There is no such thing. What I hear is the twang of the rural Midwest, the drawl of the South and the clipped nasal sound of the New Englander. When I hear what some think is a standard USA accent, it's the accent of middle Canada that graces the ears. It is the accent of the national nightly news report, the narrator of a PBS documentary. Only when crossing into French-speaking Canada and the Maritimes does one understand that even Canada has its regional accents.

As I am pondering this worldly dichotomy, Keyes has slipped out of the cockpit for drinks. When he returns, I ask, "What's going on back there?"

19

"Cap, the passengers have been fed, the movie has started and all seems well, and best of all Kenda is sending up one of the cute young things to take our dinner order."

A few moments later there is a knock on the door and a very young flight attendant enters with an offer of dinner. "OK, you guys (she is from California), the senior mama sent me up here because she said you were tired of the same old, same old, so what'll it be, chicken or fish?" We laugh in embarrassment, but of course she is right. The cockpit is still a male world. It is sexist and licentious. Avoiding the sin of sexual harassment is on everyone's mind, but in the real world it is still practiced. And what the hell, what man doesn't enjoy being in the company of a young, attractive female? Furthermore, show me the 50-year-old female flight attendant who would rather talk to a 57-year-old overweight pilot than a youthful, handsome businessman in first class!

I rest my case.

It is my company's policy on international flights that each crewmember be served a meal from separate onboard storage bins. This reduces the likelihood of contaminated food being served to all flight-crewmembers, a potentially serious problem on long transoceanic flights. On domestic flights, this is not a problem. There are no flight crew meals. Pilots are expected to plan ahead, and not get hungry. If one has poor hunger-planning skills, one can ask that a special crew meal be boarded provided, of course, that it is done with sufficient notice. The satiated pilot can then expect that a sufficient amount to cover the cost of the meal will be deducted from the monthly paycheck. You would be appalled to discover how preciously my company values its in-flight cuisine!

There is a bang at the cockpit door, the familiar sound of a female foot when hands contain crew meals and are unavailable for a more civil knock. Keyes says "I'll get it," in a tone of voice that implies, if not me, then who? Our nubile flight attendant enters and hands the meals to Keys and Gordon. I will dine last.

20

"Captain there might be a first class meal available as we had a refusal, would you like it?"

It is a sincere gesture from our youthful flight attendant and I reply, "Yes, thank you. Could you bring it in about thirty minutes?"

"You got it... thirty minutes." As she leaves the cockpit I ponder the amazing fact there is a first class meal no one has claimed and remark to Gordon: "They must all be on diets back there."

"Man this beats the hell out of domestic flying," exclaims Gordon. He is referring to the long standing bitterness between pilots and management over the lack of crew meals on domestic flights. The company argues that providing crew meals for domestic flights would add millions of dollars annually to the cost of doing business. This cost, of course, ultimately gets passed on to passengers in an increased ticket price. Besides, they say, most flights depart with more meals than necessary due to passenger no-shows, and last-minute cancellations. They make a valid point. As for the pilots, however, they recognize that flight attendants get hungry also, and few meals will make it past the growling stomach of a hungry flight attendant whose salary is miniscule in comparison to the cockpit crew. It is said that nations go to war when their population is hungry. On a much smaller scale, the same can be said of the community that exists on board the modern jet transport.

When interactions between humans with disagreements become tense, humor often defuses the situation. I remember one captain who stated superciliously, "Why hell, I don't want any slinky, skinny, cute flight attendants on my flight. Give me the older, overweight ones on a diet, cause then I get to eat." In the cockpit, humor is often mixed with sarcasm. As the story was told to me, there were three aircraft in high-altitude cruise: American Airlines at FL370, TWA, at FL350, and my company at FL330. The air was turbulent, and other flights in the vicinity were complaining to air traffic control, asking if there were any smooth altitudes reported. Air traffic control immediately began querying all aircraft in the vicinity as to what kind of turbulence they were experiencing. American replied that there were white caps in their coffee cups. TWA said that because of the rough air, the captain had just stabbed himself with his dinner fork. When my company's flight was then asked if it were experiencing rough air, the answer was, "We don't know yet, we haven't eaten."

Now, we are fully into night. The instrument panel is a montage of soft white round dials, clocks, gauges and instruments. I turn to my right, and look back at Keyes at his flight station. He is hunched over his fuel and maintenance logs, recording engine temperatures, fuel and hydraulic quantities, electrical and pneumatic loads, all taken from a panel, inches from his face, with a complexity even more spectacular than those facing Gordon or me. I turn back to my own panel, and glance down at the navigation map resting on my "Brain Bag." Quebec is now behind us, St. Anthony, Newfoundland ahead. The map is sprinkled with euphoniously named towns and villages reflecting French origins: Riviere Du Loup, Baie Comeau, Sept-Iles, Mont-Joli, Val-D'or. I try to pronounce them out loud. They do not roll easily off my tongue, and I draw a laugh from Gordon. There is little navigating to do. All of the important waypoints necessary to arrive in Frankfurt have been electronically loaded in the flight management computer. Still, I cannot help holding the map in my left hand, my thumb just under the most recent waypoint, much the same way as I did almost 35 years ago, on my first solo cross-country. Gordon jokingly asks if we are lost. I explain my odd habit, and the conversation inevitably turns to how we each got started in aviation.

"How did you get started flying?" is the second most-asked question when I meet someone for the first time. The most asked, of course, is: "What do you do for a living?" Now, I do not make it a practice to solicit this question, but inevitably when people interact, the subject of how do you make ends meet is preordained, followed by: how did you get started in your profession. With many professions, the answer to *that* question is simple; "I went to medical school or law school or business school." But 45 years ago, one did not go to airline pilot school. Besides, what people really want to know is, "What drew you to your profession," not where you were educated. They want to know what subtle influences steered you toward what was then, and still is today, somewhat an unusual career.

Gordon confesses it was all a quirk of fate, that he had no real interest in aviation. After graduating from college and facing the draft, he chose the Air Force as the lesser of evils. Gordon is a good pilot. His affable modesty rings with cover-up. Flying an airplane is not a difficult occupation if you enjoy your work. The pilot who does not enjoy flying will find the job pure hell, and will soon find himself in ill health, or in another profession. Gordon confesses he really loves the job now, but insists there was no burning desire in his youth to fly airplanes. I do not believe Gordon, but he is an honest man so I do not voice my doubt.

I am curious about Keyes. We have crewed together for several months, yet I have been hesitant to query him about his aviation past. Perhaps this is out of respect for an aviator whose beginnings trace back to Pearl Harbor and World War II. There are few airmen of his ilk remaining in the airline industry. Turning in my seat to face him, I search for just the right words but can only manage a soporific: "Jack, how did you get started flying?

As Keyes tells his story, there is a hint of lingering resentment toward the "Japs" who bombed Pearl Harbor. I have found this to be not unusual with aviators of his generation. Yet one must wonder how civil aviation would have evolved had not WW II provided the impetus, training and talent necessary for the air transport industry to thrive. There is nothing but joy in Keyes' voice, however, as he talks about signing up for the aviation cadet program while attending an aircraft mechanics trade school at the old Grand Central Airport in Glendale, Calif.

23

"They rejected me for B-17 bomber training because I was one inch too short," Keyes grumbles. "Wouldn't the people who rejected my request be interested to know I retired from Western Airlines as a captain on a DC-10 with an engine nacelle so big that a B-17 fuselage would fit inside!"

Keyes continues to tell his story, and it is one familiar to airmen of his generation, of being hired, then furloughed by Trans World Airlines, finally emerging from the heap of surplus WW II pilots, and through perseverance, and perhaps dumb luck, finding a home with Western Airlines. He then makes a statement that reflects the feelings of most of us who fly the line for a living:

"If all my life as an airline pilot were a video tape, I would hit the rewind button, and do it over again."

While it could be said that my aviation career got an unusual start with my job as a piano player, in fact it is not much different from thousands of others who dreamed of flight as young boys. There is another part of the story, however, that seems too intimate for the environs of the airline cockpit. It involves my relationship with a man who became my teacher and mentor. His name was Charley Ray, a musician and restaurateur. Most of us in our youth search for heroes. Charley was mine. Fate and good luck brought us together. My life would be forever changed.

CHARLEY RAY

"Good judgment comes from experience. Unfortunately, the experience usually comes from bad judgment." Author unknown.

The name was the only thing ordinary about Charley; his last name, Ray, being just a show business affectation. "Charley Ray's the name, show biz my game." He didn't say that, but you would have expected him to because that was Charley: musician, singer, writer, inventor, entrepreneur, barker, comic, sideman, front man, con man, lover man, superman. To this 20-year-old innocent, even more.

My first encounter with Charley occurred in his nightclub, an elegantly fading den in Long Beach, California. Perched on a bar stool behind a piano, Charley was playing a guitar-like instrument I would later understand to be an early Fender Bass. He was singing the lyrics to "But Beautiful," a popular standard nightclub song from the era of the early 50's. A tape recorder on the wall behind him provided the piano accompaniment. I took a seat at the end of the bar in front of his piano, and listened to him perform. I was not unfamiliar with his music. As a teenager I had listened to his late night jazz radio broadcast from Signal Hill, a city south of Los Angeles. In fact, I was not yet old enough to be in his restaurant-nightclub, the Twin Flame Room, being six months shy of my 21st birthday and at risk of arrest. I didn't care. I needed work badly, and having heard through the musicians' grapevine that Charley was looking for a piano player a couple nights a week, I was willing to accept the risk for the opportunity to work for him.

25

A gifted natural musician and inventor, Charley had built his fame around his personality, innovative recording techniques, showmanship and his collaboration in the development of the electric bass. Musicians and singers flocked to his Long Beach nightclub, as it had become the taproot of the music grapevine in 1950's Southern California.

In awe of his talent and very nervous, I introduced myself during his break. "Oh yeah, I've heard about you. How about playing a couple of tunes for us?"

I no longer remember what I played for Charley and his audience that evening, but it must have been good enough because Charley asked me to work every Monday and Tuesday night. The pay of $20 a night would buy groceries for a week. Charley went on to explain that he would be away from the club on those evenings, performing on the Hacienda Hotel flight to Las Vegas. Mentally counting how many groceries I could buy for $40, Charley's remark about playing the piano on a Las Vegas flight registered zero on my hungry young brain. I thought it was a joke.

Charley's diminutive stature contained a monster of energy. His smooth voice could charm the birds from the trees and the Jill's from their jeans, which he often did. On the nights when he performed I would drop in to socialize with other musicians. With a sparse crowd, Charley would have me "sit in" while he hit the streets, luring countless young women from local bars with the promise of free drinks. In no time at all, the place would be filled with young men eager to part with their cash in the interest of better male/female relationships. Charley or I would entertain, and frequently other talented musicians would drop by to sit in for a few tunes. Occasionally someone in the audience with a decent voice would be invited to sing through his secret tape recorder reverb device that could make an awful voice sound pretty good. It was one hell of a grand time for this 21-year-old.

After the first few weeks working for Charley Ray I realized that, in fact, he actually was playing the piano on an airplane owned by The Las Vegas Hacienda Hotel, and his off-hand remark was not just a statement made in jest. Completely unaware there existed an electronic keyboard suitable for installation in an overcrowded 84 passenger DC-4 of World War Two vintage, I was dumbfounded at the concept of a flying piano bar. Such decadence, in 1959, existed only in the imagination, or so I thought. In reality, it could be had for $25.00, round trip.

Twice a week, Charley performed on the Hacienda flight to Vegas, while I worked in his nightclub. One night he asked me to fill in for him on the Las Vegas flight. That evening changed my life, awakening a long dormant desire to pilot an airplane, although I was full of self-doubt that I could accomplish such a seemingly miraculous feat.

Charley had the gift of making his customers feel important. Entering his nightclub was like stepping on stage. Charley might be the entertainer but you were the star. He would ask where you lived and the next time you arrived at his club he would introduce you as the Mayor of that small unimportant city. No one cared if it were true or not. It would make you comfortable and likely to return, often. One night Harry Ross, a tall lanky former World War Two transport pilot who owned a small flying service near Seal Beach, walked into Charley's club and was greeted with the usual, "Hey everybody, let's welcome the Mayor of Seal Beach, Harry Ross." Harry was stunned into silence, and then blurted out, "Charley, how the hell did you find out, they just elected me an hour ago." What was said in jest was in fact true. The tiny, bohemian seaside village of Seal Beach had just voted Harry their Mayor. Harry owned a small flying service at the nearby Sunset Beach Airport —a half-dirt, half-asphalt, weed-covered airstrip. Charley, like me, was bitten by the flying bug, and started taking flying lessons at Harry's dust blown flight school, euphemistically named Ross Aeronautics. Short on cash and unable to subdue my

27

lack of confidence, I nevertheless followed Charley to the airport, and took my first flying lesson.

Charley's intelligence, boundless energy and ample wallet made earning a Private Pilot's License a piece of cake. There is something in the makeup of a musician that accepts the ethereal world of flight as a natural environment. With his newly minted flying license, Charley wanted his own airplane. Having plenty of money, Charley acquired a small low wing airplane called a Navion. It is no secret that aviation is mercilessly unforgiving of error. Charley's boundless energy, intelligence and money could not save him from his self. On October 16, 1959, my 22nd birthday, Charley did a really stupid thing. He killed himself flying his Navion into the ground at night. Fog covered the ground. Flying with an experienced Air Force pilot, they had set out from the club in the evening to practice instrument flying. No one knows what happened. Perhaps they misread the old WWII-type altimeter. Modern aircraft have a newer design to guard against this. But we will never really know. I was devastated. My hero--dead. The man who had taught me so much about music, provided me with a livelihood, and helped me get started in aviation was gone. Aviation is brutally unforgiving. Not many musicians die from their mistakes. If nothing else, I would take this lesson to heart.

With Charley gone, my enthusiasm for music waned. At the end of the 1950's, "Baby Boomers" chose rock and roll and rhythm and blues as their music, types that did not suit my musical taste. Aviation now had captured me completely. Perhaps the element of danger, the promise of adventure, or some primordial sense of man against nature drew my fascination. It did not matter. I knew I would earn my living flying airplanes.

"The navigator figures out the latitude and longitude. Latitude tells him where he is and longitude tells him how long he can stay there." Quote from an elementary school student of Mark Evans.

The aeronautical chart I have been using no longer serves my needs. Soon, there will be no landmarks or radio navigation stations to guide us. From St. Anthony we will proceed across the inhospitable North Atlantic via a series of way points delineated by lines of longitude and latitude, making our landfall at Machrihanish, Scotland, three hours and 37 minutes later. Gordon is plotting all of this on a chart in anticipation of our crossing. It is this chart I now hold in my hand as I instinctively look out the side window at the approaching ocean below. What do I expect to see? There is only the sinister blackness of a moonless night. Although the thought is absurd, perhaps I am looking for a competing ocean liner who is also making his crossing, wishing to share his anxieties and apprehensions with me because now we are as much of the sea as of the sky. Even our language is similar: crossing, landfall, ship, nautical miles and knots. Of course, we have our own jargon, "feet wet" when we leave the coast and "feet dry" when within gliding distance of shore. It is jargon that needs little explanation.

Keyes has been in communication with Gander Oceanic Control. They have issued us a clearance to proceed across the Atlantic Ocean via North American track Quebec. It is our requested route of flight, having been chosen many hours ago by

DiBenedetto's computer machinations as the fastest and smoothest flight path. We cannot deviate from this path without risking collision with other aircraft, therefore great care is placed in accurately programming our flight management system. The pilot not flying will carefully enter the appropriate way points one at a time. He is not to be disturbed during this process. Gordon completes this duty and then hands me the master flight plan with the quip; "O.K. Cap. You can grade my test." While I trust Gordon's abilities, I carefully check each entry against the printed flight plan. The penalty for the slightest mistake can be tragic, a fact every skilled oceanic pilot understands. It is a procedure about which no one complains. While we are not in danger of being shot down by hostile aircraft as happened to Korean Airlines a few years earlier, the specter of mid-flight collision is more than sufficient incentive to not make a mistake. In the spirit of self-preservation, Keyes, sitting between and behind us, also follows the procedure from his excellent vantage point and upon completion of the check cheerily announces, "Christ, Rick, you finally got them all right."

Once we are over water, where there are no radio stations to point the way, our aircraft will be steered by one of two autopilots, with course to steer being provided by three inertial navigation systems (INS) each costing a quarter of a million dollars. Still, they are cheaper than a human navigator, as one does not have to provide them with vacations, sick leave, and retirement benefits. Satellite navigation systems are just coming into use; however, at the turn of the 21st century, INS is still the primary means of over-water navigation. The ability to find one's way across endless oceans bestowed special powers on the great navigators of history. Drake, Magellan, Columbus and Cook, powerful men in their time, practiced their art and honed it to near perfection, gaining riches and glory along the way. It is to the benefit of humanity that navigation today has evolved into the precise world of science and mechanics. Still, there are small flaws in the system. All mechanical devices are subject to failure, if not to illness and retirement. If only two inertial navigation systems were installed, one might be faulty, therefore a third is needed as a comparator, under the assumption that a double failure is remote. Of course Murphy's Law has to be accounted for; therefore an additional system of navigation exists (aptly named if one were to get it wrong): dead reckoning.

Included on our computer generated flight plan are precise figures for heading, distance and time between each way point. If there be any art left to navigation, then it is practiced by the flight controllers who prepare the flight plans in the comfort of the company loft. In theory we can fly this artful course until the feet dry point, at which time more conventional radio navigation can be used to find our destination. I am blessed for never having to test this theory.

There is one final method of navigation, not specifically authorized or condoned, that has been in use since humanity became mobile. It is called follow the leader. In 1978, serving as first officer on one of our new flights from Atlanta to London, we practiced this procedure though luckily as leader rather than follower. As it happened, TWA was navigating with some difficulty on the same oceanic track as our flight, but at an altitude 2000 feet lower, this being standard separation at that time over the North Atlantic. It is normal to maintain a listening watch on a common frequency over water, and that is how we learned of their difficulty. Their aircraft, equipped with an older, less accurate and reliable navigation system that depended on long-distance radio waves, could be greatly affected by sunspots and aurora borealis or northern lights. Our aircraft, equipped with the very latest inertial navigation system provided reliable precision navigation. In an ironic twist, my company, flush with cash and profits had leased the very aircraft we were operating that night from cash poor and nearly bankrupt TWA, leaving them to operate with an older Boeing 707 equipped with poorly maintained Omega navigation. This irony was made much of during the conversation between their aircraft and ours. Finally they called us with the news that their navigation system had completely given up, and would we mind if they just followed us to the English Coast as they had our aircraft in sight. We of course were delighted to assist them as it could be done safely and with little effort on our part. At the same time I felt deep sorrow for the fellow airmen who had committed their fortune through no fault of their own to a sinking ship.

OVERHEAD ST. ANTHONY, TIME REMAINING 5:07

"When in doubt, hold on to your altitude. No one has ever collided with the sky." Author unknown

I cannot see the minuscule village of St. Anthony, Newfoundland. It is hidden under our aircraft. I look off to my left, toward the vast emptiness of the Canadian Arctic wilderness and see only a few meager specks of light. It is difficult to comprehend that anyone can live and survive in such a bleak and lonely landscape, yet I am told that hundreds of small villages exist, each supplying its inhabitants with their requisite share of joy and happiness, pain and sorrow. It makes one wonder if human emotion has boundaries. Who experiences the greater joy: the New York urbanite dining on Fois Gras instead of chicken, or the arctic dweller moving up to Caribou meat from whale blubber?

I must cease my musings, as it is time to climb our aircraft to a higher and more-efficient altitude. Since our departure, our three Rolls Royce engines have consumed more than 100,000 pounds of jet fuel, distilled from crude oil whose origins may be closer to our destination than our point of departure. This reduction to the weight of our aircraft will allow us to cruise at 35,000 feet above mean sea level, or in the language of aviation, flight level 350.

Gordon has made the requisite position report to Gander Oceanic Control, and they wish us a good evening and nice crossing. Keyes has reported our progress to the company using high frequency radio. In the process he has verified that our two

33

HF radios are in good working order as they will be our primary means of communication over the North Atlantic. That our HF radios are in good working order means at best we will have to repeat our transmissions, ask for repeats of receptions, sometimes scream and shout, beg, cajole and finally when all else fails, ask if someone closer to us can relay our information to the appropriate ground controller. There is no radar coverage of the North Atlantic; therefore our position reports are vital to the safe separation of the hundreds of aircraft that cross the Atlantic every evening. This miserable method of communicating is the most distasteful part of navigating the ocean, ruining our tranquility and creating a mini-crisis where there should be serenity. But it is all we have. Yes, there are promises of satellite communication, but at the turn of the 21st century, high frequency radio is still the standard. In 26 minutes we will be out of VHF radio range and will use this arcane method of communicating to report our position at 53 degrees north latitude, 50 degrees west longitude. Until then, there is blissful quiet. At least there is until Keyes speaks up:

"Captain, do you think we will see the aurora tonight?"

"Probably," I reply, not really knowing if we will or won't. Keyes knows this also. It is more thinking out loud than a query. I know of no formula that will tell us whether or not we will be treated to one of the earth's most beautiful and dramatic displays of natural phenomena. Keyes' question is more of a way to lead into a rehash of a previous flight where we experienced the most breathtaking sight of the aurora borealis one could imagine.

The routing on the evening of our spectacular flight took us high over Canada to 72 degrees north latitude, a mere 300 or so miles from the Earth's magnetic pole. The aurora, visible to us as our track across Canada took us to the higher latitudes, showed nothing unusual at this point. We in fact hardly noticed the lights as our conversation was focused on the complex requirements that restricted our aircraft to latitudes 72 degrees north and below.

Because suitable emergency landing sites are few and far between at the higher latitudes, we were going through a litany of emergency "what if" scenarios, as pilots are wont to do when things are going well. As the aurora borealis grew in intensity we could no longer ignore the spectacle filling our windshield. Our conversation languishes as each of us quietly takes in the beauty of this gift of nature with a growing realization on my part that this time it is different. I blurt out: "Jesus, I think we're going to fly under it!" To myself I am asking: Can this happen? Is it possible? I thought the northern lights were supposed to be always to the north! No one else in the cockpit is responding to my oral blurb. They are as transfixed as I. There is nothing to say —only to enjoy.

I reach overhead, and dim the cockpit lights. The waves of blue, red and green are even more intense, extending from the horizon to my left, arcing up and over our aircraft and descending into infinity to our right. It is an extraterrestrial rainbow the likes of which I know I will never see again.

Our reverie is broken by a knock on the door. It is one of the 10 flight attendants who have been sent forward to "check on the pilots." Entering the cockpit she immediately senses something is different, as we are paying absolutely no attention to her. In a moment she sees what we see, and can only say, "Oh my God." Then I hear myself say, "Yes, I think so."

"Captain, you have to tell the people about this. I'll ask Kenda if we can shut the movie off for a few moments." I am impressed with the young woman's thoughtfulness toward her passengers. I am also dumbstruck I had not given them a thought.

With the movie off and cabin lights dimmed, I make gentle turns, not enough to leave our course, but enough so the passengers can see that indeed the aurora borealis had metamorphosed into a shimmering polar rainbow of ethereal beauty. There is little cockpit conversation, each lost in thought.

"To err is human but it is not compulsory." Author unknown.

Gordon has reported our position, time and altitude to Gander Oceanic Control. We are within three minutes of our estimate. If our estimate were in error, we would have been required to immediately advise Gander of this deviation, as there are aircraft ahead of us and behind us, ten minutes in time. If necessary, Gander can command that one or all of us speed up or slow down to maintain this ten-minute separation at our next reporting point, 55 North, 40 West. Gordon also gives Gander our remaining fuel-on-board, wind speed and direction, and any pertinent information important to the safety of our flight. This is forwarded by telephone to DiBenedetto, in-flight control, or more likely his replacement, as Mr. DiBenedetto will have gone to bed by now.

We also give Gander an estimate for our next waypoint at 40 West. It will take 42 minutes to travel the 372 nautical miles to 55 N, 40 W. Gordon has the oceanic plotting chart in his lap. In ten minutes he will read our position from the INS and plot this on the chart where our course is drawn. This is the final safety check. If, after all the checking and cross-checking, a wrong coordinate has been programmed in the INS, it will show up as a dot on our plotting chart, off the planned course line.

"Captain, if you want to sit back and relax for awhile, I'll take the watch." It is Gordon's way of saying, 'Hey, there is no sense both of us staring into the blackness of the North Atlantic when one of us could be relaxing.' I won't actually go to sleep, of course, for that is forbidden. But after Gordon positions his seat so as to be able to take over the flight controls in case of autopilot failure, I slide mine back into a slightly reclining and more relaxed position. In a few hours I will be flying the approach to Frankfurt airport, with the morning sun in my eyes. It will not hurt to spend a little time away from the controls. Gordon offers an unnecessary reminder that our passengers expect a smooth landing. In the jocular spirit of the moment I offer: "You know Gordon, there are three elements to consistent smooth landings." There is a spark of interest in his eyes. "Unfortunately, no one has discovered them."

Every airline pilot is well aware that it is the last few feet of a given flight where our passengers pass judgment. It matters not what adversity may have been overcome during the in-flight passage: it all comes down to the landing. And no matter how skilled one is in the art of touchdown there will come a time when the forces of nature will humble even the mightiest. I recall just such a moment in my career.

***

1983

As we approach Newark Airport there is nothing unusual about the weather or landing conditions that would give undue concern. Not a clue that there is a surprise in store for us. In fact, the flight across the country from Los Angeles, with a Dallas/Fort Worth stop, had been smooth and uneventful. The Boeing 767 is a comfortable aircraft, popular with our passengers and with its big wing, it is not unusual to make soft, gentle landings, the type of landing that brings on applause from our customers at the end of a long, tiresome flight. It is this kind of landing that inspires pilots to perch at the exit door and fish for compliments such as, "Hey Cap'n, nice landing." And then your beaming pilot wishes you a nice day with a sort of "Aw, shucks" look that says this is the way it always is!

Not on this day.

As we neared the runway, and a split second before I expected it, our wonderful smooth-landing Boeing 767 with the big wing hit the ground. Not hard mind you, but firm enough that I found us back in the air unexpectedly. "Damn," I thought. It's not too late to save this on the rebound. But before I could complete that thought we hit the ground again, and this time noticeably harder. Again, I found us back in the air. With the end of the runway approaching faster than my brain could think, I pushed the wheel forward, and our gentle bird plopped, and sat down with a noticeable groan emanating from its various mechanical organs.

We are landed.

Although he did not say it, I could hear the first officer thinking: "The third time's a charm." In fact the silence is deafening as he averted his eyes and stared out the right side window. Somehow I sense he isn't going to volunteer to stand at the exit door wishing passengers a "nice day."

As we taxied toward the gate, my embarrassment is overwhelming. I could not stand at the door and pretend it didn't happen, nor could I pretend it didn't happen and lock myself in the cockpit. I then remembered a story told to me by a flight attendant in a similar situation. With a little self-deprecation, perhaps we might save the day. I picked up the public address microphone and announced:

"LADIES AND GENTLEMEN, THIS IS THE CAPTAIN. I KNOW YOU WANTED TO JUST ARRIVE IN NEWARK TODAY, BUT WE DECIDED TO ATTACK IT INSTEAD."

I paused to listen a moment and thought I heard a couple of laughs. Thus emboldened, I continued:

"WE HAVE JUST RECEIVED WORD FROM THE MAYOR OF NEWARK. NEWARK HAS SURRENDERED."

I placed the microphone in its holder and looked at the incredulous first officer. He started to laugh and at about the same time there is a knock on the cockpit door. The flight attendant peers in and says, "Captain, you got 'em rolling in the aisles!"

The tension disappeared.

I took my medicine at the exit door. It is a funny thing though: I received more "Nice flight, Captain" compliments than I ever got with my best grease job.

***

As I approach my final years in the air, I find myself looking back in disbelief. I have always had wanderlust but still I marvel at the technology that has allowed me to satisfy my greed for world travel. Now as I sink into reverie, my mind wanders back to my childhood during and after World War II.

1942

"Flying isn't dangerous. Crashing is dangerous." Author unknown.

If you were a child of the "Baby Boom" era, you are probably tired of hearing about World War II. Of course it is because of World War II that there are "Baby Boomers." The Second World War is the defining event of the Twentieth Century and therefore of unfathomable influence on almost all who are alive today. I suspect that most everyone born after 1945 grew up to accept travel by airplane as ordinary as electricity in our homes. Those of us born before World War II, however, grew into adulthood observing the mystery of air travel as fascinating as space travel must seem to the youth of today. To my generation airplanes were machines of war. No one I knew as a child had ever been in one, except to go to war. To this five year old boy in 1942, seeing my first airplane had all the impact of a present day close encounter.

The first aircraft I can remember seeing had rotors like a helicopter and an engine in front. I would later in life recognize it as an Autogyro, a contraption of the era half airplane and half helicopter. My brother and I were playing along the perimeter of Fairmount Park in Philadelphia, Pa., and I watched the hybrid aircraft disappear behind the tall buildings near the park edge. I didn't have time to dwell on what I saw as my brother was crying because he had fallen down and broken his arm. My mother, frantically trying to round us up to drag home and to the doctor's office understandably ignored my pestering questions about what I

41

had seen. The image has stayed imprinted indelibly in my mind to this day. I do not recall seeing another aircraft until we moved to Long Beach, Calif., in the middle of World War II.

My father, being too old and with too many children to be drafted, worked at the Long Beach naval shipyard. Our house, at 3325 Magnolia Avenue, just happened to be in line with runway 25 right at Daugherty Field, Long Beach, where Douglas Aircraft and North American Aviation, in full war production, spat out B-17 and B-25 bombers

And so the second aircraft I remember seeing as a child was a B-17 Flying Fortress, roaring overhead so close I could count the rivets. The third and fourth aircraft were North American B-25 Mitchell's, the fifth and sixth were, well, I don't remember because there were so many that day I nearly passed out in ecstasy. Like Brer Rabbit, I had found my Briar Patch. While others found the aircraft noise hell, I had found aviation heaven.

Collecting airplane photos published in the newspapers and in Life Magazine, my scrapbook grew daily in thickness. I had never seen a real pilot, but the movies and newspaper accounts told me they were special people. The war ended just before my 7th birthday. I could identify every aircraft ever publicized, a skill nearly every young boy had developed as the aviation war heroes of WWII were the idols of everyone. Soon after the war, came the Hollywood movies: *Flying Tigers, God is My Co-Pilot, Thirty Seconds Over Tokyo, Twelve O'clock High* and many, many others. It was not until 1955 and the movie *The High and The Mighty* that Hollywood filmed aviation in civilian dress.

When old enough to ride my bike out of range of my house, I pedaled the five miles to Long Beach Municipal Airport, where there were still acres of military aircraft in storage. An Air National Guard fighter squadron, equipped with P-51 Mustang fighters, made Daugherty Field their new home. Oh the sweet music of the Rolls Royce Merlin engine. There has never been a mechanical sound as symphonic and melodious as that twelve-cylinder 1400-horsepower musical instrument in full song. Even today, more than 60 years since the perfect mating of engine and airframe, thousands will gather to see and hear once again the most beautiful-looking and most goose-pimple-pumping aircraft ever built.

In 1949, we moved again, to a house farther from the Long Beach Airport, but still in line with the runways. Every evening, a pair of P-51 fighters would come over the house a little higher than at our old house, but still in full song with their rotating beacons flashing in the fading light. God, how I envied those weekend and after-work warriors who were out for an evening spin in their 1400-horsepower hot rods. Still, I had not seen nor met a real pilot. That would soon change.

My neighbor Donald had a divorced dad who, being a doctor, owned a small plane. When I found this out, I made Donald my best friend. Being more interested in Donald's father's visitation rights than anyone in his family, I would watch and wait for the doctor's '49 Ford sedan to arrive at Donald's house. Then I would slink over to his yard and pretend to be busy, while waiting for a peek at this new breed of man. I knew that if I could talk to him in person I would be able to convince him to take me for a ride in his airplane. Alas, his father seemed to hide from me. Reduced to pandering to Donald in a desperate attempt at having him intercede for me, I persisted. In time, my persistence paid off, and the day arrived when I would be taken with Donald and his brother for my first airplane ride.

I kept my disappointment at having been relegated to the rear seat to myself. I knew my impertinence and conniving had put me on thin ice. Donald sat with his father up front. Donald did not know his ass from an aileron and had no interest in aviation. Still, it was his father, not mine. I remember Donald's father with big earphones on his head speaking to some mysterious being in a language I could not understand. Then, before I could truly understand all the pre- flight activity, we ascended more like an elevator than the powerful surge of flight I had for years imagined. We flew around the airport and landed. It seemed all over before it started. There were no words of wonder from any one. No oohs and ahhs. Anxious to get on with his day, Donald's father completed his paternal duties and departed. Although slightly disappointed at his dismissive attitude, this was no ordinary event for me, but a brief moment of magic.

Many years later, I would board the Hacienda DC-4 as the piano player. It would be my second time aloft. The third time would be my first flying lesson.

1959

"Every takeoff is optional. Every landing is mandatory."

Author unknown.

A dirt road led off the main highway to Harry Ross Aeronautics. The six-by-six shack with a tin roof that extended out another ten feet to cover a beat-up picnic table comprised the operations and lounge area. A rusty Coke machine and dented coffeepot completed the décor. A few feet away, three shiny brand-new Cessna 150 two-seat training airplanes sat quietly. Harry himself, all 6 feet 6 inches of him on a birdlike frame, greeted me as I parked my new Austin Healy Sprite.

In the late 1950's, general aviation could hardly be called a robust industry. Struggling to stay in business, Harry Ross and his School of Aeronautics never passed on an opportunity to sell his service. When he heard Charley and I wax enthusiastically about flying, he suggested we come out to his school for a 20-minute lesson. Charley did so the next day and soon had his private pilot license. Being short on funds, as I had recently put all of my meager funds in a down payment on a tiny English sports car now known as a Bug-Eye Sprite, it would be a few weeks before I could come up with the money needed for a first lesson. But now in April 1959, cash in hand, I arrived ready to do something that had been a dream for most of my life.

If you are a pilot, you know the drill, the preflight inspection, the pre-start checklist, the seeming thousand things to do before you can safely become airborne. Well, Harry went patiently through each item while I stood alongside with eyes glazed over and my adrenaline pumping. I just wanted to get in the damn thing and go. And so we did, but to this day I don't know how Harry stuffed his 6 foot 6 inches into the same space that imprisoned all 5 foot 9 inches of me.

Harry was shouting instructions I never heard in the hot, noisy, bumpy and cramped Cessna cockpit; every sensory receptor in my body being bombarded with new information. I couldn't see fast enough, hear, feel or understand all the activity around me. The 20 minutes were a long second and we were back on the ground with the engine off and the parking brakes set.

"Well, howdjalikeit?" Harry asked.

"Great!" I said.

So how does one describe something so overwhelming? My mind, a confused amalgam of unrelated emotions spawning a thousand questions, could only wonder. Could I really do this? Can I really afford this? Is my life about to change? As I drove away in a stupor the answers came up, "Yes. I will find a way. And, I think so."

I sold my Austin Healy the next day and bought a Grey 1949 Chevrolet sedan with a white left front fender for $225. I stopped going to classes at Long Beach City College but did not tell my mother. I was earning about $100 a week playing the piano in various nightclubs, and paying my Mother $20 a week room and board. With no car or tuition payments (I gave absolutely no thought to insurance or taxes), this left me with almost $80 a week to spend on flying. Lessons were $15 an hour with an instructor. After soloing, I wouldn't need to pay for an instructor. This would save $5 an hour, although I would need additional dual instruction

46

before my final test. All in all I figured I could get my private pilot's license for $500. This could be earned in about seven weeks, if I ate only at home. This meant I could have my license in two months. I had it figured out to the day and the dollar. And you know what? My calculations were damn near perfect.

A few days after selling my beloved Bug Eye, I returned to the airport for my second lesson, scheduled to last about one hour. Harry Ross introduced me to Ed Rice who would be my permanent instructor. My initial disappointment at not having Harry as an instructor turned to relief when I saw that Ed's 5-foot-4-inch build was going to provide us with a hell of a lot more room in the cramped Cessna cockpit. Besides, Ed being a former Marine F4U Corsair pilot out of WWII and Korea figured to be a better stick and rudder man than Harry. (Stick and rudder man meaning a person with a natural aptitude for flying).

I spent every day at Harry Ross Aeronautics, Sunset Beach Airport, Calif. I would arrive in the morning and leave in the afternoon. Being obsessed with and possessed by aviation, I lost all interest in everything else. When I wasn't flying, I studied books on navigation and manuals on aircraft rules and regulations. Even though I would only fly one hour or less each day, the hours spent hanging around the other aviators were like a free ground school. This would be my new college education. My degree would be my private pilot's license. After several weeks and seven hours and 39 minutes of flight time, Ed Rice got out of the airplane and sent me off by myself. To those of you who have done it, I need not tell you what it is like. To those who have not, I can only say that I can think of nothing that will change the way you look at yourself and your life more than flying an airplane from the ground through the air and back to earth by yourself and on your own.

55 NORTH 40 WEST, TIME REMAINING 3:59

"Ladies and Gentlemen, we've reached cruising altitude and will be turning down the cabin lights. This is for your comfort and to enhance the appearance of your flight attendants."

An in-flight announcement from the cockpit of an unidentified Continental Airlines flight.

Gordon's position report to Gander Oceanic has shaken me out of my reverie. Gander has requested we contact Shanwick Oceanic at 56 North, 30 West, as they will be the controlling agency until we approach the Scottish Coast.

I have trouble with the name Shanwick. I know it is an amalgam for the cities of Shannon, Ireland and Prestwick, Scotland. I also know that at one time Prestwick was the controlling agency for Eastern North Atlantic flights. I also know that in the early days of transatlantic flying, Shannon became the first stop, as aircraft of the day had not the range to fly further. I am ashamed to realize I do not know whether we are speaking to someone in Ireland or Scotland. I vow to rectify this embarrassing revelation and to further investigate what political intrigue ensued to cause the creation of such an inharmonious sounding name for a non-existent city.

There is a knock on the flimsy cockpit door. Keyes checks the peephole to verify that it is indeed one of our pleasant-looking

49

flight attendants, and not a would-be axe murderer-hijacker who possibly is unaware one swift kick will open the door.

She has come forward with coffee but lingers to chat, for she is one of those rare females who are fascinated with the magic of flight. And why not? We sit in the best seat in the house, with a view of the world unsurpassed except perhaps by the astronauts.

"I will soon have my commercial license and instrument rating," she proclaims proudly. "And then the next time the company hires pilots I intend to be in front of the line." While she won't be the first female to do so, she will surely not be the last.

The relationship between airline pilots and flight attendants has been the subject of many books, newspaper articles, movies and especially jokes. Let's face it. What young man wouldn't want to work in an environment of beautiful young single ladies, well educated and selected from the cream of the available crop? It was not that many years ago that career choices for women were limited and an airline job was a way to meet successful men on board the aircraft. Businessmen, at that time, were the bulk of the paying passengers. It is no secret that the work environment spawns more love affairs than any singles bar or dating service. It matters not if it is the corporate office, a hospital, a factory or an airline cabin, wherever the sexes cross paths, romance will inevitably thrive.

There is however, a special relationship between the captain of a flight and the flight attendants, be they male or female and it has nothing to do with sex.

Flight attendants are the frontline of passenger service. Certainly the gate, reservation and ticket agents play a very important role, but the attitude of the in-flight service providers is often the difference between a passenger's perception of a flight being good or not so good. Airlines hire young women and men who have those qualities of patience, sympathy, good humor and a touch of caring and concern for others. All of these sterling qualities can be dampened and discouraged by a captain who is insensitive to the needs and concerns of the cabin attendants. The job of the captain is primarily to see that the flight is operated in a safe and timely manner. However, his responsibility as overall commander of a crew of as many as eighteen or as few as three, is very important to the well-being and profitability of the company who employs him.

The ideal flight is one that offers the opportunity to meet your fellow crewmembers in a non-frenzied environment to discuss possible problems in advance and review emergency procedures. Weather, special passenger and catering requirements and connecting flights, are just a few of the many items that should be discussed. This, however, is not the way it always is. The reality of bad weather, late flights, mechanical and personnel problems often makes the pre-flight briefing consist of a few mumbled introductions with each crew member ducking into his or her work area in an attempt to leave on time. In 1981, I served in command of just such a flight:

As I boarded the aircraft in Dallas/Ft. Worth, scheduled departure time had faded into memory. Rotten weather on the East Coast delayed all departures and my flight, along with many others, arrived late at DFW. I did not see any cabin attendants, as they were busy tending to our inconvenienced and unhappy passengers. The first officer and I proceeded to the cockpit to run the pre-flight checklist. As we completed our checks, a call on the interphone to the flight attendant completed the required safety briefing. While the flight to Denver was normal from the pilots' viewpoint, the flight attendants were nearly overwhelmed with irate passengers who had missed their connections. All communication with the passenger cabin was by interphone. After landing in Denver, the passengers deplaned and the flight attendants followed them off to get something to eat, as they had not eaten since leaving the East Coast. By the time I had completed the post-flight checks, the aircraft was empty. I had not seen a single member of the in-flight service crew.

Our departure was in less than an hour so I remained on board to take a short nap in the last row of first-class seats. As I had slumped down in the seat, no one saw me napping there as the cabin crew boarded after their meal. In short order the four female flight attendants were chatting together in the forward seats and one began telling a joke that would burn the ears off any normal male. I cannot repeat all of it here but the hero of the joke seemed to be a fictional airline pilot for Air France who, with much passion and persuasion, began putting some moves on a stewardess in his hotel room during a layover. The hero of this comic tale, Captain Pierre Le Blanc, renowned as a famous French Air Force fighter pilot now turned ordinary airline pilot, could not contain his enthusiasm as he kissed and fondled his love from neck to breasts to navel and ever lower until finally at the critical anatomical point, he whipped out his Zippo cigarette lighter and set fire to her.... "Pierre! Pierre," she screamed..."What are you doing?" Here you must understand this story is being told with an impeccable French accent, including the punch line: "When Captain Pierre Le Blanc —famous French fighter pilot— goes down, he goes down in flames!"

I could not contain myself as I sat up. The look of horror on the sweetest, most innocent face imaginable cannot be described. The blush of her red face made a nice contrast to her blond hair. As she began to apologize, I had to cut her off, as the passengers were entering the aircraft. Frankly the joke was one of the funniest I had ever heard.

As I sat in the cockpit before departure, it occurred to me that she might think that I had no sense of humor and might report what she meant to be a private conversation, to her superiors. I had no such intention. However, this could put her in a poor mood for the flight home, so to put her mind at ease I thought of calling her on the interphone to let her know that I, after all, also had a sense of humor. I instead got a better idea.

As we waited at the runway end for our takeoff clearance, I picked up the public address microphone and made our required pre-departure announcement like this:

"LADEEZZ AND GENTLMENZZ, ZEES EEEZ CAPEETAN PIEIRRE LE BLANC. WHEEEL ZEE FLIGHT ATTENDAANTS PLEEZ BE SIT-ED FOR ZEE TAKING OFF. MERCI!"

Not a single passenger complained about surly flight attendants or about pilots with funny accents.

Keyes is again busy with his fuel and maintenance logs. Our erstwhile new hire quietly watches over his shoulder, hoping to gain some special knowledge that might give her a leg up on the competition. She is not needed in the cabin. Most passengers have long been asleep. My mind wanders back again to the early days. Gordon remains on watch.

COMPULSORY MILITARY SERVICE

"Experience is the knowledge that enables you to recognize a mistake when you make it again." Author unknown.

Growing up in the era of compulsory military service posèd a dilemma for every young man. I could go to college and defer the draft, or just join up and get it over with. In any case I could expect, at the very least, a two-year bite out of my life. It would be difficult to start any type of decent career until the obligation to my country was completed. Not believing I would ever be smart enough to fly an airplane, I nevertheless decided to join the Air Force reserves while still in high school. After all, there were many other jobs one can do and still be around aviation. Besides, I could be fulfilling my military obligation while attending college. And who knows, I thought, maybe I will finally understand the higher mathematics that seemed so all important to being a pilot. While I could not foresee that it would be a wise move, it in fact turned out to be just that.

With my private pilot's license in hand and my confidence soaring, I decided to work toward my commercial license and flight instructor rating. I knew this would be expensive, but along the way toward earning my private pilot license I discovered something about myself that would ease the financial burden. Self-study suited my style. Give me a book and the time, and I could learn almost anything. With no time-consuming and expensive ground schools to attend, I passed the written exams and two months later, the Private Pilot flight test. In order to gather the required hours for the next level of ratings, I purchased a one-sixth interest in a Piper Tri-Pacer and flew the hell out of it, much to the dismay of my airplane partners. Within one year of soloing, I had accumulated enough flight hours to pass the flight tests for commercial pilot with instructor rating. The impetus for all this expended energy was an incident just after receiving my private license.

With my newly found confidence, the idea of flying jet aircraft in the USAF re-entered my mind. Although I did not as yet have a college degree, the Air Force allowed you to take the flying aptitude tests and the officers' candidate school tests, but with a higher grading standard than a college graduate. At March AFB in Riverside, Calif., I began three days of testing. The first day I passed the flying aptitude test with a score so high that, according to the test director, I could have given some of my score to the five who failed, and they too would have passed. The following day, however, I received my comeuppance, swift and brutal. The officers' candidate school tests did not care if you could fly or fart; it just wanted to know whether or not you could do algebra, geometry, trigonometry and calculus. After all, an officer in the USAF must be more than just a pilot. I failed miserably and was told in no uncertain terms to go back to college and learn these subjects. For me, there would be no third day and I returned home devastated.

After a few days of feeling sorry for myself, and regaining some of my lost confidence, I began the crash program to get my commercial and instructor's license. The idea of returning to college for remedial mathematics held little appeal, especially after learning that a friend, Ron Adams, who had passed all the Air Force OCS tests and gone to flight school, was sent home with all his classmates. The Air Force had cancelled all pilot schools for the foreseeable future. After all, there were no wars going on, and the defense budget had been cut. My dream of flying jets with the USAF appeared doomed. I consoled myself with the thought that being in the wrong place at the wrong time is perhaps a message: I should look to civil aviation to find my future.

The day after I passed my flight instructor check ride, I was hired by Harry Ross as a part-time instructor with a salary of three dollars per flight hour. My first student, a young man who just wanted to see what it was like, had no inkling of my lack of experience. I took him up for a twenty-minute demo flight and when I returned, Harry wrote me a check for one dollar. He then reached in his pocket and pulled out a dollar bill, gave it to me, and said, "Don't cash that check and you can forever say that you still have the first dollar you ever earned flying." I still have that check, but the dollar bill bought my lunch.

Besides earning a small income, instructing meant I did not have to pay for all of my flying, as I could log the time instructing as regular flight-time. And it was all about flight time, because I needed a total of 1,200 hours of flight time to be eligible to earn the Ph.D. of aviation, the airline transport pilot rating, commonly called the ATP or ATR. I also had to be 23 years old. I was 22.

Now that military flying seemed less and less likely as a way to gain flying experience, I sought every avenue available to gain that valuable flight time. I would take friends for short trips in my one-sixth of an airplane; we would share the expenses and I would log the time. By hanging around the airport on my days off there would inevitably be someone whose airplane needed ferrying to another airport for maintenance, which I would do for free. Again I would log more flight time. I began studying for the ATR written test, although lacking the flying time necessary to qualify.

Trigonometry, calculus, advanced algebra—surely I would have to face this in my studies. Where was it? As I studied for the ATP the most advanced mathematics I encountered concerned weight and balance. This required no more than high school arithmetic. Even computing the brake horsepower of a radial engine, given the displacement and fuel consumption, could be accomplished with a few spins of an aviation circular slide rule. Trigonometry consisted of a few simple wind vectors, again easily done on the backside of the venerable E6B aviation slide rule. (We called them computers back then.) In fact the most difficult part of preparing for the ATP test was the myriad of federal rules, then called civil air regulations. While tedious and numerous, they were learnable. So then, I had built a mountain out of molehills. Thank God.

I was feeling pretty good about myself around this time, perhaps even a little cocky. I had a bit more than 500 hours flight time and was beginning to fancy myself a latter-day Chuck Yeager. Any experienced pilot will tell you this is a dangerous time in a pilot's learning curve. Someone had forgotten to tell me.

My coming of age began when offered the opportunity to fly a new Piper Commanche 260 to Phoenix where I would pick up a passenger and take him to Springerville-Eager Airport in the White Mountains north of Phoenix. The Commanche, a low wing, fast aircraft with a wing design similar to a WWII fighter, would test my limited skills, as I had very little experience in this type of airplane. I knew it was not built to fly into unimproved, short or rough runways. The gravel runway at Springerville-Eager, perched at an elevation of 7,500 feet above sea level, required special knowledge to safely operate there. The possibility we would be landing after dark, only added to the complications my meager experience would have to contend with.

Despite some brief misgivings, I jumped at the opportunity to take the flight, though a small knot in my gut said, "Be careful." I knew I was challenging my skills, but my ego and overconfidence shucked off the internal warning, resulting in a near disaster.

After an uneventful flight to Phoenix, I arrived only to find my passenger had not. Hoping we would be able to conduct the flight in daylight, my butterflies returned when I realized we would be completing our flight in the dark, over high mountains with no moon to an airport I had never seen, in an airplane I had hardly flown. Still, my ego could not be subverted by my mounting doubts.

After takeoff we climbed immediately to 11,500 feet to clear the mountains north of Phoenix. The Commanche had no oxygen equipment on board, so no thought was given to its use. Besides, I had flown many times at even higher altitudes with no apparent ill effects; or so I thought.

I had been told in Phoenix that some of the runway lights were not working in Springerville-Eager, and when we arrived overhead I could see that the runway looked very, very short. Concluding that half of the lights were out on one end, I had only to figure, which end was lighted and which end was not. A muddled conclusion in hindsight, brought on by mild hypoxia as a result of our flight at high altitude.

Circling the airport, I descended to about 30 feet above the runway and decided that the runway extended past the working lights and we could land in the direction we were now headed. Pulling up to go around for the approach, I was surprised to hear the stall warning indicator sound two or three times. This meant I was too slow and needed to increase my speed. I did so and maneuvered to put us on final approach so as to touch down where the lights began.

As we touched down going very fast (landing speed is much higher at 7,500 feet above sea level because of the thin air), I noticed immediately the barbed wire fence reflecting my landing lights was strung across the runway just beyond the runway lights. Try as I might, I could not stop the airplane before arriving at the fence. Rather than hit a fence post head on, I aimed the aircraft nose between two posts. We hit the barbed wire at about 50-mph with a sickening thud. Thank God, the terrain on the other side of the fence was as smooth as the gravel runway. Finally stopped, I sat there stunned, thinking: "Where in hell did that fence come from?"

After the dust settled we got out of the airplane and found several hundred feet of barbed-wire fence wrapped around the wings and propeller. Flying into an unfamiliar airport, in the mountains, at night, with a high-performance airplane, is difficult even for an experienced pilot. I had no business accepting this flight with my limited experience. Pride goeth before ... well you know the rest.

Assumptions can kill. I had no business assuming, just because I did not see a fence, the runway extended past the operating runway lights. In fact, we landed in the middle of the runway, not at the beginning. Flying at high altitude without oxygen can dull your senses, even for short periods. Landing at a high-altitude airport after such a flight is absolute folly. Perhaps this is why I took no account of the wind direction, and landed down wind, exacerbating my attempts to slow down the plane.

Finally, a commercial pilot owes it to his customer to not put that customer's life in danger. A commercial pilot owes it to his customer to use good judgment and not let pride and ego stand in the way.

The 1960's version of the FAA slapped my hand, gave me a lecture about high-altitude airports and offered this advice. "You learned a valuable lesson without killing yourself. Don't ever forget it"

I have not!

The humbling experience of Springerville-Eager made me determined to straighten up and fly right, to measure the thickness of the ice I chose to skate on, to mind my P's and Q's and a few other pearls of wisdom drilled into my head by my mother.

Despite the black mark on my record, Harry Ross still thought I had the skill to be a good flight instructor and recommended me to a friend of his for a full-time instructor position. And so I went to work for Bob Marks Aviation in Torrance, Calif., instructing in a Luscombe 8-A aircraft.

The Luscombe 8-A could be a real bitch to land in a crosswind, as it had a very narrow landing-gear of conventional configuration, what we now would call a tail-dragger. Bob Marks was a former WWII P-47 fighter pilot who got shot down just after logging 500 hours flight time. But Marks was no fool, and before he hired me he sat quietly in the right seat while I demonstrated what little proficiency I had in the tiny Luscombe. Taxiing back to his hanger his only comment was, "Well I guess you'll do, but watch your ass because this little bugger will turn around and bite it!"

I could hardly believe my good fortune at being fully employed with a steady paycheck in the industry I loved most. The $100.00 a week salary would leave little pocket change at the end of the week, but it didn't matter, because now I would be building hours at the rate of 80 to 100 hours a month. On my day off, I worked toward my instrument and instrument instructor ratings. This caused the near demise of the Long Beach Municipal Airport control tower, not to mention the FAA inspector and me. This time however the fault would not be mine.

Long Beach had the last remaining low-frequency navigation range station. This system, invented in the 1930s to help Lindbergh-era airmail pilots find their way, used a series of Morse code, A's and N's. If you were on course, you heard a solid tone. If you were right of course, you heard a dot dash, left of course a dash dot. Because this antiquated system remained operational at Long Beach, I must demonstrate proficiency in its use to qualify for an Instrument Rating, even though it had been replaced with more modern navigation systems elsewhere.

On the day of my check ride, after having passed all the other required maneuvers for my instrument rating, it was now necessary to accomplish a LF radio range approach with an FAA flight inspector acting as observer in the right seat. We were flying my venerable one-sixth of a Piper Tri-Pacer, it being equipped with the necessary radio. The FAA inspector, an elderly, kind and mild-mannered gentleman, handled the communications with Long Beach Airport tower as I would be preoccupied using the earphones to identify the dots and dashes of the radio station. We approached runway 30 at Long Beach, and feeling pretty good because all I could hear was a steady tone, I figured we were right smack on course. I wore a hood to keep me from seeing anything outside the Tri-Pacer, therefore simulating instrument flight conditions. In fact, however, we really were in IFR conditions as we headed directly into the afternoon sun with the infamous and dense Los Angeles Basin smog obliterating all forward visibility. The FAA inspector could see only straight down, and to the side of our flight path. I could detect a touch of concern on his part that, perhaps we should postpone this test to another day when he said, "Oh hell, lets get it over with. I can see straight down, and can tell if you're on course or not."

As we continued toward the runway with a steady tone in my headphone he said, "I think you're to the left of course. You'd better come right." This did not jibe with what I was hearing from the radio and I hesitated to change course. "Dammit," he said. "Come right!" Again, I hesitated to change heading, as the trust of your instruments is a pillar of instrument flying. "I've got it. I've got it," he cried. "You're way off to the left." I let go of the controls as ordered while he banked steeply to the right. I took off my hood knowing I had failed the test, only to stare in shock as the tinted windows of the Long Beach Airport control tower filled our windshield. "HOLY SHIT," we said in unison, as we both cranked the wheel hard left. There were more than a few moments of silence as I let him fly the Tri-Pacer out of the traffic pattern and above the smog level where visibility was again plentiful. "Jesus, you were right after all," he said. "That was my fault. I'll call the tower and apologize. I hope there aren't any weak hearts in that control tower."

I breathed a gigantic sigh of relief as he said: "Don't worry. You passed OK, but I ain't never gonna do one of them again no matter what those assholes in Washington say. Fuck em!"

I firmly believe I am the last person on earth to attempt a low-frequency radio range approach. The merciful shutdown of the Long Beach low frequency radio range shortly after my nearly disastrous check ride went unnoticed by most of the aviation community. The system that had guided thousands of aircraft to a safe landing, but whose difficulty in use caused unknown numbers of passenger deaths, was finally replaced with the modern and safe Very High Frequency Omnirange (VOR) navigation system in use to this day.

Good riddance!

I knew my time with Bob Marks' small operation would soon end. If I were going to get a job as an airline pilot, I simply had to get more experience in larger and more sophisticated aircraft. In 1958, Pan American Airways began Boeing 707 service across the Atlantic to London. Shortly after that, United and American began domestic jet powered transcontinental air service, soon followed by TWA, Delta, National, and Eastern Airlines. Although the number of jet transport aircraft was increasing in 1961, Douglas DC-6, DC-7 and Lockheed Constellation propeller driven aircraft were still operating the bulk of domestic travel. The impact, however, on pilot employment began to be felt, as each jet airplane did the work of three or more of the older non-jet airplanes. This did not bode well for my hopes of an airline career as I began hearing tales of layoffs and furloughs. In any case, I would not be discouraged and continued my quest for the all-important experience I needed, by going to work for Evelyn "Pinky" Briar at Tri-Cities Airport, near San Bernardino, Calif.

Pinky Briar was a rarity in 1961—a female commercial pilot. Formerly a WAAF (Women's Auxiliary Air Force) veteran of WWII, she ran a lean mean charter operation with a reputation of being a difficult employer. While finding her reputation well-deserved, I nevertheless reveled in the fact I had my very own Beechcraft Bonanza assigned to me to do nothing but charter flying six days a week. Icing on the cake came in the shape of a Cessna 310 twin-engine aerial hotrod that she entrusted to my burgeoning skills. It was important for my future career that I amass as many multi-engine hours as possible. My salary of $500.00 per month made the perfect strawberry atop the icing. I had never seen so much money.

Flying for Tri-Cities Flying Service can only be described as a young pilot's dream. Working for Pinky Briar however, became pure hell. Nearly every day I would have a charter flight up or down the California coast, or to Las Vegas, Nev., and nearly everyday Pinky would find fault with my excessive flight time or excessive fuel burn for that particular flight. I could do nothing right. She knew every foot of the California landscape and would tell me exactly which tree, rock or ranger station to fly over for the shortest possible distance. She also knew exactly how many gallons and pints of precious aviation fuel a Bonanza burned to get there. But she made money in a business where few others could.

One day, as I departed with a Las Vegas charter, she took off just behind me destined for Los Angeles. Her Bonanza, a new N model, climbed about 10 knots faster than my older M model and she soon pulled along side and called me on the radio. "Hey, do you know your step is not retracted?" she asked. The passenger boarding-step, designed to retract automatically with the landing gear, had failed to do so. Since I could not see the boarding step, and there being no indicator on the aircraft that would tell me it was not retracted, I gave a now-how-would-I-know-that-shrug and turned toward Las Vegas. That night the faulty step was overhauled, and soon my times and fuel burn were as good as, and sometimes a little better than her own. My pride returned. Her bitching stopped.

Just before being employed by Pinky Briar, I worked for a flying school in Riverside, Calif. One of my students, a secretary for the Riverside and San Bernardino County coroner, wanted to learn to fly to please her boss, the County Coroner. The coroner, a pathologist with no interest in flying himself, bought a twin-engine Piper Aztec, and paid for his secretary's flying lessons. He needed an airplane to cover the incredibly vast desert area that was his responsibility, and figured his secretary could do this as well as anyone. While no easy task, the secretary persevered and by God, she did it and actually went from student to commercial pilot with all her flying done in the twin-engine Aztec. Boy, was that expensive.

During the time I labored for Pinky Briar, the doctor would occasionally hire me to fly his Aztec when the weather was marginal for his secretary, as she was not instrument rated. On one occasion I was invited to observe him perform an autopsy on an unfortunate 22-year-old Marine, who had mysteriously died. I did so, but only that one time, and thereafter I remained at the airport, an environment far more to my liking. Despite my squeamishness, the kind doctor took a liking to me, and allowed me to use his Aztec for my airline transport pilot rating check ride. With more than the required 1,200 hours flying time, and now being 23 years old, I passed my ATP rating written exams and flight test. I now had the highest ratings required by the FAA to be a pilot.

Even though I had only once been in the cockpit of a transport-type aircraft (as the piano player) I now had all of the licenses to be one! Of course, this did not really qualify me as an airline pilot, as there remained the not insignificant hurdle of earning a type rating in a particular transport aircraft. During this era, only an airline could offer this kind of training. So then, my over-rated rating did not mean much except that I could meet at least the government requirements. However, one incident made every drop of sweat, blood and tears expended to earn this rating more than worth the effort. This incident brought me a little revenge on those miserable Air Force testers who flunked me because my calculus was crap. I had my pound of flesh from those arrogant bastards. Then again, perhaps I am over-reacting.

In order to fly into certain Air Force facilities, it was necessary for me to obtain a special security clearance. A large portion of Tri-Cities Flying Service's business was transporting special, highly secret missile parts from Southern California aerospace companies to Edwards AFB and occasionally Vandenberg AFB. I relished these assignments, as I got to visit and see the newest and fastest Air Force jet aircraft. I was still envious of the military pilots and not at all sure I hadn't made a mistake not going back to school to learn their damn higher mathematics. Still, I also knew that time was running out for me and going into the Air Force at this point was going to make it impossible to get a job with an airline. The scuttlebutt said that if you weren't hired by your 27th birthday you were just dead meat as far as the airlines were concerned. And so I resigned myself to the more practical of my desires; to be employed with a major airline. And yet, I could not get over my bitterness at having been turned down over what seemed to me such trivial shortcomings.

The incident began with my assignment to transport a small electronic box to Vandenberg AFB, located along the California Coast north of Los Angeles. When I arrived at Vandenberg, a thick fog bank lay just off shore and threatened to sweep over the entire coastline. Just as the duty officer signed for the secret box, the threat became reality, and within minutes dark clouds enveloped the airport, completely obscuring visibility in all directions. The duty officer said, "You better check with meteorology before you depart because I think the field is closed." The meteorologist confirmed the duty officer's suspicions, and added that he did not think it would lift until the next day. I did not relish the wrath of Pinky Briar when I told her that one-third of her charter fleet was grounded at Vandenberg AFB, so I began to wrack my brain for the applicable federal air regulation that would allow me to depart.

As a civilian, I understood the regulatory quirk that allowed me to depart in any weather conditions I chose as long as I was not carrying anyone or anything for hire. But was it safe? Yes, I surmised, because the fog was only obscuring the runway, and once airborne it was no threat to safe flight. Only in the event of total engine failure would danger become an issue. In other words, it was my ass and no one else's. The Air Force base dispatcher did not see it my way.

"Young man," he said, "This is a military base, and no one departs here until I say so. So why don't you just have a seat in the ready room, and wait for the fog to lift!" I persisted, "You mean there is absolutely no circumstance that would allow an aircraft to depart in this weather?" His look of condescension was total. "Yes," he said impatiently. "We do let Air Force pilots with special-rated green cards and *airline transport pilots* sign their own dispatch release, but no one else."

"So then," I said, "If I have an airline transport pilot rating, I can sign this dispatch release and go?" His smirk began to fade as he stared at me, and said in a voice rapidly losing its arrogance. "Yes, eh, that's correct."

I met his stare and slowly, ever so slowly reached toward my billfold, and laid it on the dispatch counter, opened to the little two-inch by four-inch card, protected by its yellowing plastic cover but plainly visible for all the world to see, and spelled out in impeccable U.S.-government English, and in all capital letters that:

WILLIAM LAURENCE IPPOLITO HAS BEEN FOUND TO BE PROPERLY QUALIFIED TO EXERCISE THE PRIVILEGES OF AIRLINE TRANSPORT PILOT.

He held my stare as I said, "Yes, I have that, sir."

And so our U.S. Air Force duty dispatch officer, temporary ruler of the kingdom of Vandenberg, looked down at my certificate of competency, the small piece of cardboard that made me the equal of the Air Force's very best, and slowly pushed the clearance paper across the counter toward me and said with resignation: "Sign here, and have a nice flight."

After takeoff, the sun never looked so bright, or the ocean so blue, and the future so promising. For the very first time I had the feeling that my career as an airline pilot was going to happen. "To hell with the Air Force," I thought. But in truth, I still envy every one of them.

Despite my personality clashes with Pinky Briar, I could not have chosen a better way to gain valuable flying experience than flying for Tri-Cities Air Service. Charter work afforded the opportunity to visit many out-of-the-way places and I spent much of my time in the California deserts. Those were the days of the X-15 rocket plane, an aircraft that actually produced the first true astronauts, as they would fly over 50 miles high. The military operated a test site north of Las Vegas where the noise of rocket planes and sonic booms were heard by almost no one. Transporting the operating personnel and maintenance crews to these remote stations, where they manned ground monitors that would relay vital information about the test flights, challenged my flying skills. It was no easy matter finding these secret stations and then selecting a suitable nearby dirt road where a safe landing could be made.

One memorable destination, the Goldstone satellite tracking station operated by the Jet Propulsion Laboratory in the northern Mojave Desert, could not be found on any map. Pinky told me how to find it, and explained that on arrival I would find only a telephone booth that I would use to call my passenger. As I approached Goldstone Dry Lake, I could see two parallel painted black lines defining the landing area on the immense expanse of glaring white, hard packed dry lakebed. Without the two lines, depth perception would be non-existent and finding the ground a dangerous guess at best. After landing, I taxied toward the only man made structure in view. It was just as Pinky described to me earlier: a standard 1960 era telephone booth complete with folding doors for privacy. The doors seemed redundant, there being not one sign of any human ever being here, with the exception of the telephone company and perhaps someone with a bucket of black paint and a straight edge. Acting like Cary Grant in an Alfred Hitchcock Movie, I dialed the number given me and soon, across the desert, I could see a trail of dust as a car arrived to take me to the station.

For 30 minutes, we drove across the desert when suddenly, as we rounded several bleak desert rocks, a giant antennae dish appeared. Dumbfounded, I gaped in amazement. This could only exist in a science-fiction movie, I thought. My many questions elicited few answers. My orders were to pick up my passenger and depart, and not be so nosey. I did just that, but oh what a revelation to bestow on this innocent twenty one year old who thought he knew so much.

California's benign weather is ideal for light aircraft flying. During the year I worked for Pinky Briar, weather rarely affected our flights, except for the occasional reduced visibility caused by coastal fog and Los Angeles smog. However, the mountainous terrain in California presented a challenge to both the novice and the experienced pilot, especially during the winter, when weather fronts often presented high winds, rain, snow and ice. During just such a period Pinky fired me.

I had been assigned to fly into Lone Pine, California, an airport on the eastern slopes of the Sierra Nevada mountain range near Mammoth Lakes, Calif. My weather check indicated high winds, and possible icing conditions, at which time a knot in my stomach told me this is not a good day for flight in a small plane. Since I had never been to this area of the Sierra Nevada Mountains, I had no feel for the risks involved, given the poor weather. Remembering my humbling experience in the mountains of Arizona, and determined not to screw up again, it seemed prudent to explain to my passenger that perhaps waiting another day would be a wise decision. There was no need to confide in him that my ambition to pilot airliners would be in jeopardy if another black mark were added to my shaky record.

Pinky Briar blew her stack when I told her my decision. She did not mince words, and ordered me to take the flight or go home and find another job. As I looked at my hapless passenger, I could see his total confusion and embarrassment. I said to him, "Pinky will take you. I've just been fired." I went home.

The next day Pinky called and began chewing me out over the telephone. I couldn't believe her anger persisted this long. Besides, hadn't I been fired? What the hell is this all about, I thought? I listened as she ranted and raved on and on and when she completed her tirade I could only surmise that I had been given one more chance. Incredulous at this turn of events, I accepted her "nother chance" and went back to work the next day.

After a week of rather cool relations between us, Pinky called me to the office with a flight to Las Vegas. There, in the office, stood the passenger I had abandoned to her a week earlier. I said nothing except "hello," and turned to head out to the airplane with my passenger following. After we got in the plane, he turned to me, and said: "I just want you to know I specifically requested you for this flight. I am never going to fly with that crazy woman again—she nearly killed us!"

Hmmm, perhaps I had learned something after all.

A few months later, another job opportunity came my way: the chance to co-pilot a DC-3. Having gained all the experience I could working for Pinky, the time had arrived for me to move on to something new—something that would really impress my future airline employer; that something would be the mother airliner of the fledgling airline industry, the Douglas Commercial Model Three.

In 1932, the world's airlines needed an airplane capable of earning its operators a profit, and no more airplanes made with sticks, fabric and baling wire. Passengers were demanding all metal aircraft, with comfortable seats and heated cabins. Passengers wanted more speed, so a trip across the continent would not take more than a day. Jack Frye, president of TWA, laid out this plan to Douglas Aircraft Company and Donald Douglas built him the DC-2 that could carry 14 passengers at almost 200 MPH. The president of American Airlines said something like, "Wait a minute, we want the airplane to carry 21 passengers so we can earn a profit." So Mr. Douglas built him the DC-3 that was no faster but could actually earn a small profit for the airline with the additional passengers. Until the DC-3 came along, airline profits could only be made through the benevolence of the U.S. government, by carrying subsidized U.S. airmail. With the DC-3, profits could be earned carrying both passengers and mail, earning real returns for airline investors. Consequently, no airline in the world could afford to be without the Douglas Commercial Model 3. Therefore, to be an airline pilot during that time meant you were a DC-3 pilot.

My opportunity to pilot a DC-3 came about because a California entrepreneur thought in 1962 there was a public need for DC-3 service on short intra-state routes. He could not have been more wrong. His error, however, became my opportunity, and when I answered the "experienced pilots wanted" ad, he told me where to go to get the ground school training I lacked (at my own expense) and to come back when I had completed my training. So off I went to Burbank Airport for two eight-hour days, studying the nuts and bolts of the DC-3 at Fowler Aviation, who then awarded me a certificate of completion.

Certificate in hand, and hired by Air Oasis Airlines at $350 per month, my new employer sent me off to sell our services to local travel agents up and down the Southern California coast. I hated this part. I wanted to fly, not sell. One of my first visits, to San Diego's Lindbergh Field, introduced me to Delta Air Lines; a small southern company only recently awarded transcontinental routes to the west coast. While I failed to convince the agent working the sales desk to utilize our services, she impressed me with her vigorous promotion of her own employer. Frankly, I had never heard of her company until that day and considered the only "real" airlines were United, American, TWA and Pan American. The intensity of her attachment to her "airline family" left an indelible mark on me as I weighed the choices I might have to make in the near future.

My new employer soon realized I was bereft of sales skills and in an act of mercy scheduled me for three takeoffs and landings in the DC-3, thus qualifying me as a DC-3 first officer. (Oh my! How things have changed since then.)

The DC-3, to my eyes, lacked the graceful lines of other, less capable, aircraft of the era. Perhaps because of the standard landing gear it appeared squat and dowdy. Standing next to it, however, it looked really, really big compared to the small light planes I had been operating. One could just see the faded outline of "Braniff Airways" bleeding through the coat of paint hastily applied to hide its history. Appearances aside, here is a true airliner, I thought, capable of handling the worst that Mother Nature could throw at her, and still delivering her passengers safely to their destination. She looked tired, and long in tooth, but still gracious and forgiving. Standing in front of the high nose pointed skyward I could understand why WWII aviators nicknamed the DC-3, "Gooney Bird." Still, in 1962, there existed no better aircraft to transport 21 people and additional cargo over short distances. Unfortunately, we could not find 21 people who wanted our scheduled services. The business stayed alive for a few months by hauling work crews back and forth from Long Beach to the California offshore islands of San Nicholas and San Clemente, where the military operated secret ordinance testing sites. Soon, however, the company folded when the investor recognized his mistake. As for me, again unemployed, but with 100 hours of DC-3 co-pilot time preciously recorded in my logbook, the time had come to look for another job where my new skills could be utilized.

Seeking out other companies who operated the DC-3, I found Mercer Enterprises, at the Burbank Air Terminal. Paddy Mercer, the owner, crammed 32 seats into his DC-3s and chartered them up and down the coast. The pay, $20 per day, gave no consideration to the number of hours flown.

Most of my flying for Mercer consisted of short distance charters to California horse racing tracks, or the occasional haul of freight for an auto manufacturer. On one charter however, we carried the entire Lawrence Welk Orchestra to San Francisco and I was stunned to recognize one of my college friends among the Welk musicians. His surprise was equal to mine and he hoped I flew airplanes better than I played the piano.

Paddy Mercer, a nice guy to work for, understood the economics of the charter business as well as anyone. He understood the business could not support high cost new aircraft so he sought out cheaper aircraft that could do the job; therefore his aircraft were old and weary. Besides the DC-3, he actually had one of the last remaining DC-2s in existence, a former Eastern Airlines' relic, designed to carry 14 passengers. Paddy crammed 21 seats in the space designed for 14. The DC-2, with a slightly narrower fuselage and a smaller wing than the larger DC-3, looked so much like its bigger brother a novice could not tell them apart. The DC-2 however could fly ten knots faster than the DC-3 because of its smaller size.

I knew the time marked in my logbook as DC-3 would enhance my chances of landing a job with a major airline. I could not have foreseen however that it would be decisive. Soon enough I would be thanking the gods for bestowing on me the blessings of the world's first real airliner, the DC-3.

LOOKING FOR A JOB

"Stay out of clouds. The silver lining everyone keeps talking about might be another airplane going in the opposite direction."
Author unknown.

The time spent flying for Air Oasis and Mercer Enterprises not only gave me valuable experience flying the DC-3, but also contact with pilots who had flown for other scheduled airlines. Looking for a job as an airline pilot was a little different than looking for employment in traditional careers — there were no help wanted ads in the local newspapers. I learned from other pilots to study industry publications where rumors and stories often pointed to job opportunities. Today, I suppose, this would be called networking. Unfortunately, in 1962, due to industry consolidation, there were more laid-off airline pilots than pilot jobs. The jet airliner could do the work of three piston-engine types, thereby reducing the number of pilots required. In addition to the surplus of pilots, the airline tradition of hiring only the young made things even more competitive. Most airlines had age limits of 27. A few, believe it or not, insisted you be no more than 25. That just happened to be my age in 1962, and the thought that I was already over the hill became traumatic. In actuality, however, the law of supply and demand determined hiring age, and that law soon reversed as baby boomers came of age. My youth (ahead of the boom) placed me in good company at the time.

The thousands of surplus pilots of WWII had migrated to other occupations. So too, had the Korean War Veterans. This development, combined with the dearth of military trained aviators, soon caused an unforeseen pilot shortage. My generation, of which there were few, led the baby boomers into the jet age! Of course, I had not the slightest inkling of this phenomenon, as I figured if there is a job out there, I needed to find it before someone else did. Thus, I pursued every rumor, every whisper, every outright lie, if any truth could be found in it, in my quest for employment with a major scheduled airline. In hindsight, I could have sat on my duff for two years, and then been recruited like today's hotshot computer whiz with a masters in e-commerce. Luckily, I didn't do this as the lost two years would have cost me dearly in seniority and opportunity.

I wrote to every airline in the world. Most foreign carriers still employed pilots trained in the USA. My apartment looked like an international mass marketing boiler room. Every three months I updated my résumé. While most of my inquiries received replies, none led to employment. In a strange way, the rejections bolstered my confidence, as none of my potential employers laughed at my résumé, and none required military flying experience. In fact, I found I met all of their stringent requirements.

Toward the end of 1962, I could sense the winds of change. Industry scuttlebutt reported that American, TWA, United and others had recalled their furloughed pilots. Frontier (then a major regional airline), Delta and Northwest were considering hiring new pilots. The one airline I most desired to work for, however, Pan American World Airways, seemed mired in political and financial intrigue. Pan Am, along with most international airlines, almost overnight converted to jet aircraft, thus displacing hundreds of pilots who now were in competition with me for available pilot positions. Nevertheless, time now worked for and not against me, as the demand for air travel increased. I began to get positive responses from the flurry of résumés exported by my personal PR department.

The first airline to respond favorably to my multiple requests for an interview, United Airlines, asked that I report to their Los Angeles personnel office. While not hiring at the moment, they professed, they were interviewing candidates for future flight officer positions. This being my first experience applying for a job with a large corporation, I had no idea what to expect. Surprisingly, the young man who interviewed me seemed only slightly older than me, and furthermore, not a pilot. I couldn't understand the logic of having a non-aviator perform this function. His questions seemed more oriented toward hiring an office clerk than the future captain of a Boeing 707. He expressed disappointment at my spotty work record, implying that I couldn't hold a steady job. I became rattled, and was unable to find the proper words to explain the importance for me to constantly seek new employment, therefore furthering my experience level. His lack of knowledge regarding aviation and technical matters shocked and embarrassed me. How in the hell can they put this idiot in charge of hiring pilots when he didn't know a U2 from a urinal, I thought? The interview did not go well. Nevertheless, he sent me to a testing room where, for the first time in my life (but not the last), I stood face to face with the infamous MNPI personality test.

1.   I believe I am an agent of God. *True or False.*
2.   When out for a walk I try to avoid stepping on the cracks of the sidewalk. *True or False.*
3.   When confronted with a mistake I have made, I often find others to blame. *True or False.*

What the hell kind of whacko is this outfit hiring? Where are the questions about density altitude, weight and balance, visibility minimums and aerodynamics? Am I in the right department? Is this an airline or a psycho ward?

Later, of course, I learned from my more experienced compatriots that this is just part of the testing to weed out "weirdo's," and that later on I would be interviewed by real pilots asking reasonable questions. Nevertheless, the whole experience left a bad taste, and I concluded that I wanted them even less than they wanted me.

I approached my next job interview, with Frontier Airlines, with far more caution and anxiety than the interview with United. I did not really want to work for Frontier, as they only flew short hops with small piston-engine and turboprop aircraft. Although they would later merge with several other regional airlines, and eventually become part of today's US Airways, I felt their future limited. Besides, I still had my heart set on a carrier with international routes. Nevertheless, desperate for employment, I found my way to Denver where a flight instructor immediately stuffed me in a Link Trainer to see if I could fly. No useless questions or stupid testing, just get in and "show us your stuff." Full of self-confidence, I did, and immediately crashed!

Let me explain the Link Trainer. The Link trainer could be called the first aviation simulator used to teach pilots "blind flying" or what we now call "instrument flying." All pilots hated it as it did not handle like a real airplane, and would humble the most skilled aviator. Once inside with the lid closed, it was fly or die. My early demise on the premises of Frontier Airlines resulted from being set up by the instructor to drive home a point. Sealed in the "box" (what we called the link trainer), I was told to check the approach chart, then proceed to the outer marker and hold. (Translation: Go into a holding pattern.) As the lid closed on the box, I noticed the altimeter reading 5,500 feet above sea level. The link trainer would immediately begin losing altitude when first turned on if you did not begin flying it right away. I needed to study the approach chart to find the proper holding altitude, and thinking I had plenty of altitude above the ground, I allowed the link trainer to start descending. That is when I crashed, because we were, of course, in Denver, and after all, it is accurately called the "Mile High City."

"We don't want you to ever forget you will be flying in mountainous terrain," the flight instructor told me. "That is why we set you up like we did. Now let's try it again."

I got it right the second time, and after the written tests, Frontier Airlines offered me a job as first officer on a CV-540 turboprop with a domicile in Billings, Montana. I liked the people at Frontier, and though not my first choice, I accepted their offer. Told to report for training in 30 days I boarded the return flight home with mixed emotions. While I would soon be employed with an airline, the position fell short of the dream I had dearly worked towards. While my disappointment grew on the flight home, it would soon be dispelled by the incredible good news waiting my return.

I almost dropped the telephone when I heard the words: "We are currently interviewing pilots for possible employment with our company. If you are interested, please come to my office in Atlanta for an interview. Our office hours are … " Yoweee! Yes. I will be right there. Please don't change your mind. When is the next flight? What's the guy's name I'm supposed to see? Horace Messer? OK Horace, I'm leaving right now!

No, not Pan Am—they wouldn't be hiring again for several years—but an airline worthy of consideration, Delta Air Lines. Delta had real airplanes, a fleet of DC-8 and CV-880 jets, transcontinental routes, and a sterling reputation for employee relations. No, they did not fly overseas, only Pan Am and TWA were allowed to do that, but they were not hiring pilots. I recalled the positive attitude and optimistic outlook voiced by the ticket agent I met in San Diego. I remember her confidence that her company would one day be one of the biggest world airlines. Something told me this would be the right choice, and so I boarded their Atlanta nonstop flight that very night. Sleep be damned. (Who could have imagined in 1963 that Pan American World Airways and TWA would not exist in 2002.)

Horace Messer, vice president of personnel, wasted little time. He gave me a yellow cab voucher, and sent me to the office of Dr. Janus, the in-house psychologist for testing. With wild gray hair, inch-thick glasses, and a monster of a moustache, the rotund and broadly smiling Janus seemed straight out of central casting.

"Come in, young man, come in. Please have a seat and tell me all about yourself." Janus pointed to, of all things, a rocking chair. I sat, and tried not to rock. I told him about myself, including all the jobs I'd had, and why I chose to have so many, all the while remembering the miserable little shit at United Airlines who belittled my work record. When I finished, Janus said, "My oh my, isn't that remarkable? You never lost sight of your goal. I like that. This company needs people like you." Stunned and blushing, I could only mumble a "Thank you."

So I proceeded to undergo tests, tests, and more tests, until finally Janus said, "OK, young man, go back to the airport and see Joe Mangum—he's our pilot interviewer." I did as told.

Joe Mangum might have been one of Delta Air Lines original crop duster pilots. He certainly looked the part. A line pilot now retired from flying, he had the final say on hiring, and aware of that fact, I sweated bullets. His piercing eyes poured over my logbooks. He said little as he flipped through the pages. As he approached the last records, his eyes brightened and he exclaimed, "What's this? DC-3 time? You flew DC-3s?" A moment passed before I realized the significance of his comments. This ancient birdman, this grizzled old veteran of line flying flew DC-3s. To be an airline pilot in the 1930s, 40s and 50s meant you were a DC-3 pilot. The DC-3 is Joe Mangum, not just an airplane. "Yes sir, and a little time in the DC-2 as you can see," I responded.

"Well, I'll be god-damned. It's about time we got some real pilots to hire. All I see these days are B-47 and B-52 pilots. What the hell do they know about airline flying? So what did you think about the old Gooney Bird?"

What did I think about the DC-3? I think if I answer correctly, I am going to have the job of my dreams. I think if I tell you the Bird is the most beautiful, magnificent flying machine God ever created, you are going to hire me. If I tell you I will cherish forever every moment I spent at the controls of the Bird, you are going to bless me, and reward me like no man has ever done before. That's what I think of the Douglas Commercial Model 3.

And so I told Joe Mangum, veteran of the skies, ancient pelican of the air, master of the DC-3, all these things.

Leaving Joe Mangum's office, I could not contain my elation over the turn of events. Walking the long terminal corridor toward the departure gate I wore an ear-to-ear grin that had fellow travelers staring in wonder. On each side of the corridor sat rows of DC-6 and DC-7 aircraft, mated to their aluminum stairs. At the far end sat the shiny new DC-8 jets, connected by modern jet ways. Everywhere there were passengers boarding or de-planing. Passengers hugging and kissing in greeting, others offering tears and handshakes in departing, children and adults, babies and businessmen, parents and grandparents, lovers and leavers. If all of existence were to have just one center, that center would be an airline terminal, and that terminal would probably be located in Atlanta. Soon, I knew I would be a part of this. Though not yet official, as I had to wait for the confirming letter, I knew Joe Mangum, and I knew a fellow DC-3 pilot would not let me down.

"We are pleased to offer you employment … report to the training center … April 1, 1963, at 8:00 a.m." With so few words, a life is transformed.

I can think of no other occupation as dependent on the mother company as that of an airline pilot, for better and often, for worse. In 1963, the government controlled the airline industry, both politically and economically. Congress awarded airline routes as political spoils. The Civil Aeronautics Board regulated fares. The

government promoted and protected the nation's air carriers—
regardless of their financial performance. So, it didn't matter how
hard you worked or whether your company is productive and
innovative. No matter how inefficient your company performed,
in 1963, the government would not let you fail. Government
subsidies, and monopoly routes, kept the most poorly managed
airlines afloat. In this controlled environment, labor unions
instituted strict seniority rules. With almost no interchange of
employees between airline companies, a cradle-to-grave mentality
developed within the industry.

In 1978, the Airline Deregulation Act changed this practice
by freeing the airline industry from economic regulation. Some
airlines failed, but most thrived. Still, even at the turn of the 20th
century, your company remained the mark of who you were.
Government benevolence and union seniority played more
powerful roles in shaping my career than any superior flying skill I
imagined I possessed.

After receiving the offer of employment from Delta Air Lines,
I wrote Frontier Airlines and thanked them for considering me for
employment. Left unsaid was the fact that a better life awaited me
than the one they had to offer. I also had one more flight
scheduled with Mercer, in the DC-3. It nearly ended in disaster.

Captain Hugh McHenry commanded my last Mercer flight.
For this I was grateful, as his easy going, affable but competent
persona made our flights together a pleasure. At the age of 40, he
was too old to seek employment with a major airline. In fact I had
never heard him express remorse over this fact, as he seemed quite
happy piloting DC-3's for Mercer. We both looked forward to our
return to Burbank, as Paddy Mercer—who bore no ill feelings
towards me as I left his tiny operation for greater glory—had
arranged a going-away party. Paddy boasted he was proud one of
his "graduates" was good enough for the "big boys". En route to
Los Angeles, where we would discharge our passengers before
proceeding to Burbank, a thunderstorm stood in our way.

Incredible as it may seem, on this day, March 15th, 1963, the rarest-of-rare phenomena occurred: thunderstorms over the Los Angeles Basin. We approached LAX from the west, over the ocean, and were cleared to land on runway 7 right. Light rain fell and the wind blew hard out of the southeast. I was grateful Hugh was flying, as I had never landed the "3" in such a strong crosswind. The windshield wipers—seldom used in Southern California—were worn and useless. We touched down right wing low, right wheel first, but as Hugh brought the wings level, the plane slid left with the wind, and in an instant we were straddling the left runway lights—one gear on the runway, the other off. With a magnificent effort, Hugh wrestled the aircraft back to the runway as my heart pumped adrenaline. I could do nothing but watch, and keep my hands to myself. As we rolled to a stop just off the runway, he said, "How many runway lights do you think we took out?" I had no idea, still in a catatonic state. However, the LAX tower said nothing. Either they didn't notice, or we miraculously missed them all.

We discharged our 32 passengers, and took off again in quieter conditions for the ferry flight to Burbank Air Terminal. The quieter conditions would not last. Burbank Airport lies at the foot of the California coastal mountain range. The cool Pacific air from the ocean colliding with this range caused violent updrafts, thunderstorms and heavy rain. It could last for days, and, in fact, did. Hugh once again took the controls, and I did not protest. As we entered the area of heavy rain just five miles from the runway, every worn seal, every slight gap in the wheezy-old bird let in torrents of water. Water poured on my head, flowed onto my lap, ran down my legs, and filled my shoes. The turbulence was so bad it made speaking into the radio mike almost impossible. When I did, I halfway expected to be electrocuted. I imagined I could hear the soul of our worn-out war horse screaming, "Enough, already, I am supposed to be retired in California, not bouncing around in some god-damned Midwest thunderstorm!" How many storms like this had the old bird survived in its past life with Braniff? Beginning to wonder whether I would survive to enjoy the career that awaited me just five miles away, I began a little prayer. "Please God, get us to the runway safely so I will never have to fly in a piece of shit like this again!" I meant no disrespect to our DC-3. It had served aviation and mankind well, but it deserved better.

Back slaps and congratulations greeted me as I stood dripping wet in the tin shack that housed Mercer Operations. I thanked Paddy and Hugh, and a few others who had dropped in to see the "guy that had it made" on his way. There would be no sense of sadness, only relief.

APRIL FOOL

"The probability of survival is inversely proportional to the angle of arrival. Large angle of arrival, small probability of survival and vice versa." Author unknown.

It is April 1st, 1963, and I have been told to take the fourth seat in the front row. The seats are actually standard school desks, with a half-table that flaps over for writing. The fourth desk from the left indicates my seniority in the class. There are 21 others behind me. It is small comfort to know that if the airline were to let me go, they would have to furlough 21 pilots before me. The fact that it's April Fool's Day contributes to my insecurity and disbelief. I have heard too many disaster stories of layoffs, furloughs, firings to take anything for granted. My good fortune still seems like fantasy. I fully expect the tall, thin, curly-headed messenger with an almost incomprehensible Southern drawl standing before us to announce: "I am sorry to inform you that this has been a big mistake, and in the spirit of the day you may all go home." Instead I am bowled over with the following words:

"Mah name is Frost Ward. I'ham yoh instructah. Y'all are heah 'cause this company needs you. Y'all have been hiyed to be captains of oweh new jets, but yoh fust job will be as flight engineahs on oweh existin' piston-engine fleet. Y'all have been selected from an eleet group to fill empty cockpits just waitin' foh you to complete this cawse. If y'all will open yoh books to page one we'll get stahted."

85

Eight hours a day, five days a week, 25 "eleet" young men no older than 26, and no younger than 22 studied the mysteries of the radial engine, the Rube Goldberg intricacies of hydraulics and electrical systems, the mechanics of aerodynamics and the tedium of record keeping. The pay, $350 per month with medical benefits, and a one-week vacation after employment one year, would not cover my current living expenses. In two months, if I passed my FAA flight engineer test, I would gain a raise in pay to $450 per month. First, however, I would have to master the language of the south—and learn to eat grits.

On the third day of class, we were asked to show our FAA licenses and medical certificates to Horace Messer, the vice president of personnel. One week before we started class, news broke nationally that Eastern Air Lines hired an unlicensed pilot in 1947. Though skilled as an aviator, having flown bombers in WWII, this pilot hadn't completed the formalities of becoming a licensed civilian pilot. And for 15 years, no one at Eastern bothered to check his credentials. Finally, a zealous FAA inspector noticed the discrepancy when the errant aviator tried to upgrade to captain. Incredible as it may seem, until this day no one had ever asked me to show my pilots license. Perhaps it is because people thought that if you were crazy enough to fly airplanes, surely you must have the proper license. Sloppy record keeping could result in millions of dollars in fines for the nation's air carriers. Hiring an unlicensed pilot did not fit my company's agenda.

In airline pilot heaven all ground instructors are skilled and competent. The average airline pilot would not survive the alternative. The complexity of modern aircraft requires many hours of instruction and self-study, the kind of study many pilots find boring, tedious and of course, necessary. A born instructor, Frost Ward arrived with wings both figuratively and literally. As both a licensed pilot and ground instructor, Ward could teach a rock to roll over. I suspect he often thought of our brains as just that. His patience seemed endless, especially if you were from the south and could understand him. Frequently, I would ask him to spell a word I didn't understand, thereby subjecting myself to humiliation and ridicule. To the three Yankees in the class (myself included), he showed no mercy, and often referred to me as the "Eyetalian" guy. For the most part, I absorbed and understood Ward's lectures fully until one day, in a late-afternoon fade, with my eyelids sinking towards my knees, I awakened to the word "WHY," seemingly being shouted in my face. Startled to realize I had momentarily dozed off and thinking I had been asked a question I had not heard, I sat up straight and confessed I did not know the answer.

Oh the humiliation! Ward looked at me, and then looked out at the class, and said: "Did y'all heah me ask this dumm Yankee a question?" Then looking at me he said, "What ah said was you will get a shock from this motah if you touch this whar."

The bantering, all in good fun, served to release the built up tension that fear of failure brought to the entire class. I began to realize this company really did need us, and Frost Ward's job was to make sure we learned everything he had to teach. He didn't cut any slack for anyone—the chilling reality of that came a few days later when one of my classmates suddenly no longer occupied his assigned seat. Ward said nothing, except, "He is no longer employed by this company."

Toward the end of the first month, I received a distressing letter and newspaper article from my mother, reporting my old friend Harry Ross had gone missing on a flight from Salt Lake City to Long Beach. I found it difficult to accept that the two men most responsible for my start in aviation had died while piloting their aircraft. Ten years passed before hunters near Cedar City, Utah, stumbled upon Harry's wreckage.

There would be no graduation ceremony when we completed the course and passed our FAA tests. Nor would we be awarded any medals—we were not in the military. Instead we got private industry's highest honor: a pay raise.

FLYING THE LINE

"Always try to keep the number of landings you make equal to the number of takeoffs you make." Author unknown.

My company owned 10 DC-8 and 17 CV 880 four-engine jet aircraft in 1963. It had far more DC-6, DC-7 and Convair 440 reciprocating engine powered aircraft than it had jets, as did every other major airline during that time. Lacking suitable short-haul jet aircraft, the DC-6/7 and Convair 440 aircraft took up where the long-haul jets left off. Four ancient C-46 Curtis Commandos, complete with Chinese script imprinted on various parts revealing their past life, were utilized as freighters. The C-46 hauled everything that could not fit in the cargo hold of our passenger jets and more importantly, it could ferry a good jet engine to an aircraft down with a faulty one.

The position of flight engineer, often called a second officer, did not require pilot skills. The position came about when government aviation regulators decided that aircraft with complex, reciprocating engines needed someone in the flight crew exclusively devoted to keeping those engines operating smoothly. In the early days this job often required mechanics trained to do repairs in remote outposts. In later years, the complexity of jet aircraft with their air conditioning, pressurization, hydraulic, pneumatic, electrical and fuel systems, still demanded the full attention of at least one crewmember. But, since few jet aircraft flew to remote outposts anymore, repair skills were no longer needed. So, many airlines instead began hiring and training pilots as flight engineers. The flight engineer/second officer position became an entry-level cockpit position. Not inconsequentially, this also prevented union problems during that time when there were more crews than there were cockpit seats.

The DC-6 and DC-7 were similar aircraft with the DC-7 having a longer fuselage and more powerful engines. The second officer's duties included starting the engines and controlling them during most phases of flight. While the captain or first officer moved the throttles in the direction desired, the second officer fine-tuned the power settings, keeping the propellers synchronized. During icing conditions, the second officer manipulated carburetor heat, cowl flap settings and de-icing equipment in a complex ritual designed to keep each of the four engines running smoothly.

Those who have witnessed the wonder of a 2,400-horsepower R-2800 Pratt & Whitney radial engine during startup know the glory and spectacle of radial engine start. It's more like the opening bars of a symphony than the mundane rotation of aluminum and steel. If you are among the unblessed, I will try to put the music and miracle into words:

First, the flight engineer engages the starter on the overhead panel by squeezing his right thumb on the safety switch toward his right-hand middle finger, which is squeezing the actual starter switch. This begins propeller rotation. When the captain or first officer counts six blades passing a given point, he calls out, "Six blades." The flight engineer then activates the ignition boost by squeezing his right-hand index finger toward his thumb while activating the fuel prime with his ring finger. The left hand meanwhile is reaching almost to the cockpit floor to bring up the fuel mixture when the engine is running on prime. It is more like conducting a symphony than starting an engine, as the ring finger skillfully adds prime fuel in just the right amount, bringing in the bass notes of solo cylinders firing in a pizzicato opening bar, while the left hand calls forth the full chorus of 18 pistons, firing evenly in a deep and harmonious roar. Flames pour from the exhaust stacks as blue smoke seeps from every cowling seam. Then the wind created by the propeller seems to cleanse the engine, and soon there are only beautiful chords held in sustain as the engine settles into normal idle. Oh what music! I wish you could have heard it, and seen it.

After several flights as an observer, my company deemed me proficient enough to trust me on my own. My initiation into the exciting world of big time commercial aviation began on June 12, 1963, with an Atlanta-to-Orlando round trip in a DC-7. The captain, one of our most senior pilots and nearing retirement, had passed up the opportunity to fly the new jets. Nearing the age of sixty, the training involved for qualifying in the new era aircraft would have taken him past his birthday. I figured he must have been born before Orville and Wilber Wright made their historic first flight in December, 1903. While I remember of course, being very nervous, the one memorable thing I recall about that night was the permanent pot of ice tea the captain kept on the glare shield. Every 20 minutes or so, one of the two stewardesses on board (flight attendants had not yet been invented) entered the cockpit to replenish the shiny stainless steel pot with fresh ice and tea. This was not requested, rather it seemed ordained.

The remainder of that first summer on the line passed without mishap. The stunning spectacle of summer thunderstorms and insufferable heat lent balance to the pleasure of being surrounded by the attractive Southern girls serving our passengers. It is no accident that the majority of Miss Americas come from the Southern states. They are gorgeous. With the arrival of winter, however, I had my first real scare.

In December, while conducting an ILS (Instrument Landing System) approach in cloudy, rainy weather to St. Louis' Lambert Field, I experienced my first taste of serious winter weather conditions. When winter comes to the Midwest, it marches in relentless three to five day cycles as the Arctic weather fronts roll south from Canada. We had not encountered any icing conditions during our approach and none had been forecast. Unbeknownst to us, however, a layer of freezing air had settled over the area, trapped under an inversion. With both pilots' attention on their flight instruments, I monitored, and made small adjustments to the engine power. A competent flight engineer can help the pilot fly by adjusting the throttles to keep the airspeed at the desired number. We could see nothing but white cloud and light drizzle. Approaching 200 feet above the ground, I stole a glance through the windshield, expecting to see the runway. Instead I could see nothing but a solid coating of ice obliterating any view outside the cockpit. Before I could say anything the captain called out, "Let's go around," my signal to apply full power to the four engines. I attempted to do so, but the throttles would not move. In disbelief, I pushed harder against the four levers that controlled the engines — still they would not move. By now the captain had brought the nose up to keep from hitting the ground we couldn't see. Now the airspeed began decreasing rapidly as our power was insufficient to sustain even-level flight. It took only a microsecond for me to realize our throttles had frozen solid. Being only seconds from a collision with the ground, and not knowing what else to do, I grabbed all four carburetor heat levers, and pulled them up to the full-on position. Almost simultaneously, the captain reached overhead, and pushed all the de-ice and anti-ice switches full on. We were only too aware that the engines were not producing much power, and therefore not much heat. Would there be enough to free the throttles? I pushed with all my might, and suddenly they broke free. The engines screamed in protest at such brutal treatment. Every engine gauge rotated past its safe operating limit. It could not be helped, with death only feet away. Ten thousand horsepower, unleashed from their frozen harness, screaming in agony, hauled the DC-6 skyward. The engines were dangerously over-speeding, and I could detect the beginning of detonation, a condition that can destroy an engine in seconds. While the captain skillfully balanced airspeed and altitude, the power must be reduced or our engines will self destruct. Adding carburetor heat at such high power settings caused the cylinder head temperatures to go off the limits of the gauge, so I began to reduce the heat and finally the power as the captain built up a small reserve of airspeed and altitude. As the DC-6 settled into a stable climb, I quickly scanned the oscilloscope that monitored each of the 144 spark plugs in the 72 cylinders I had so abused. Apparently we had done no permanent damage. Thank you Mr. Pratt and Mr. Whitney for building in a small reserve.

The first officer managed to feign calmness as he reported the icing conditions to the tower and requested another approach. Little conversation took place between us as we completed our second approach, this time with every de-icing system running full blast. When our passengers had deplaned a stewardess asked, "Hey, what was that all about?" I said simply, "Well, we just couldn't see it the first time." It seemed to satisfy her curiosity.

Most airline pilots have a good sense of humor. Some are downright devilish, and like to pull practical jokes on their fellow crewmembers. The working environment of the airliner, in the early days, with its male-dominant cockpit crew, and female-dominant cabin crew, especially lent itself to hi jinks. In the adolescent years of the airline industry, the flight attendants, then called stewardesses, were mostly very young women just out of school, and working their first real adult job. The cockpit crews, on the other hand, were salty veterans of WWII and the Korean War, and thought these young ladies were fair game for a little prank or two. I confess to being a party to more than a few very hilarious incidents.

My company used the DC-6 for short routes, as there was not yet a suitable short-range jet airliner that could do this. A typical route segment, for instance, might take us from Dallas, Texas to Shreveport, La., to Jackson, Miss., then Birmingham, Ala., and finally Atlanta, Ga. Often these flights were conducted at night, and with few passengers. Cargo and U.S. Mail were our main revenue. These conditions allowed far too much opportunity for shenanigans, as the stewardesses had little to do.

93

On just such a flight, while conducting an exterior inspection before departure, I noticed two caskets being loaded in the belly cargo compartment. A recently hired and very young stewardess also noticed the two caskets and asked, "Are they going with us?" in a very tenuous voice. I confirmed her unpleasant suspicions, and thought I detected goose bumps and mild shivers overcome her.

After takeoff, I related my encounter with our new "stew" to the co-pilot, and I swear I could hear the mental gears grinding, as he was a noted prankster. Shortly, he pulled out a fake, rubber bloody severed hand from his flight kit. (God knows for what reason he kept it there.) I sensed the hatching of a prank.

Just behind the flight engineer's seat, the DC-6 has an exterior cargo door leading to a cockpit cargo area. At the next stop, our fun-loving first officer closed this door on his fake bloody hand, leaving it resting on the cockpit floor. After takeoff, and when everything had become serene and with only the dimmest red lights glowing in the cockpit, he called our young victim forward with a request for coffee. Standing directly behind me she could see little as we discussed our unpleasant cargo peacefully in repose under the cockpit floor.

With his right hand, which she could not see, our fiendish first officer, began knocking on the side of the cockpit wall. Knock! Knock! Knock! "What the hell is that?" we all asked practically in unison. As we furiously pretended to examine our flight instruments, the unfortunate young lady became agitated and nervous. The steady knocking continued, slowly but methodically. Knock! Knock! Knock! This was too much for our nubile new hire. "I'm going back to the cabin," she nervously announced. "Wait a minute," cried the co-pilot, "You've got to help us find where this noise is coming from. Get a flashlight and look around the cargo compartment behind you."

I handed the poor thing a flashlight, and she began searching the compartment behind her.

"Check the floor," I guiltily offered.

I will never, ever forget her scream when her flashlight discovered the bloody hand.

She threw the flashlight at me as she ran out of the cockpit, slamming the door so hard it bent the hinge.

We did not get any more coffee that night.

A few weeks later on a similar flight, the first officer left his seat to use the head located in the forward passenger cabin. Before he returned a stewardess entered the cockpit and stood behind my seat gazing outside at the tranquil night landscape. The stars appeared as almost a mirror of the earth below. There were few passengers on board and the low, melodious droning of the engines and the dim cockpit lights tended to put one in a meditative state. Few words were spoken as our stewardess relaxed, sipping a cup of tea, seemingly in a state of melancholy, perhaps reflecting on a lost love. She did not notice the vacant first officer seat, hidden from her view by a bulkhead. She also did not notice when the first officer quietly re-entered the darkened cockpit and stood behind her.

On the verge of waking her from her reverie so the first officer could get to his seat, I noticed he held a small flashlight on his chin and face, like we used to do as kids on Halloween. I could not resist the opportunity, and said "OMIGOD! WHATS THAT BEHIND YOU?" Turning to face him, she screamed and then threw her cup of hot tea at the hideous illuminated vision.

I decided to curb my appetite for pranks after that incident as the more senior first officer subsequently displayed a certain coolness toward me. But what the hell, he had the flashlight, not me.

The eventful year of 1963 wrapped up in dramatic fashion for me on Christmas Eve, while we awaited takeoff clearance at the south end of Washington National Airport. As I sat in the DC-7's engineer seat, I could see in a southerly direction a National Airlines' Lockheed Electra approaching the runway. Our takeoff clearance would come when he safely landed and turned off the runway. In the dark of night, all I could see of him were his many landing lights. Following his progress, I could just make out the shape of the fuselage as he passed abeam our nose. Something did not look right. Momentarily thinking the lights were playing tricks on me, it appeared as though his landing gear remained retracted, and not extended. It was no trick. I screamed, "CHRIST, HIS GEAR IS UP!"

Ken Fisher, the first officer, also could see the coming disaster, and wisely picked up the microphone and starting yelling, "YOUR GEAR'S UP, YOUR GEAR'S UP, YOUR GEAR'S UP!" We both watched in horror as his landing lights reflected against the back of the propellers spinning only inches above the ground. A crash seemed inevitable while Ken repeated his frightened warning. Just when we expected sparks and disaster, instead we watched the nose quickly rise, and the Electra shoot like a rocket skyward. We breathed a sigh of relief, took off, and headed home for Christmas.

Later that night we got a call from air traffic control indicating that the National Electra pilot had reported his landing gear "down and normal," and would we like to comment. Realizing the Electra pilot had chosen to cover his ass with the FAA, we said, "No sir, perhaps we were mistaken." We, of course, knew we were not. And as pilots like to say to one another when somebody screws up: "Hell, I made a mistake once, but then I realized I was mistaken!"

Two years after this incident the FAA, under pressure from the Air Line Pilots Association (who knew better than anyone the limitations of human memory), made it mandatory that all transport aircraft must be equipped with a warning horn that sounds when the landing gear is not down and landing flaps have been selected.

THE END OF AN ERA

"The propellers are only there to cool the pilots: If you don't believe me watch them sweat when they stop." Author unknown.

It seemed to me that my airline had two divisions. The first, equipped with a modern fleet of jet transports, proudly carried the company logo coast-to-coast and border-to-border. Sophisticated computers generated reliable weather reports and flights were planned for maximum economy and passenger comfort. We coddled our jet passengers with air-conditioned boarding tunnels called jet ways. In-flight meals grew in sophistication and coffee could be fresh brewed on board. All of my company's energies and resources were directed toward the goal of an all-jet fleet, second to none. But until profits allowed and aircraft manufacturers designed and delivered the new aircraft to accomplish this goal, there remained the other division—the one I worked in.

My division featured the last of the piston-era aircraft. Our passengers boarded their flight on aluminum stairs, exposed to the weather, grateful for the barrel full of umbrellas on the bottom step. Our coffee, drawn from large stainless steel thermos jugs, might have been brewed hours before serving. We balanced our meal trays on a lap pillow, and the meal arrived complete with complimentary cigarettes and toothpick. We produced our own flight plans, with paper, pencil and the venerable E6B circular slide rule, in other words, no different than pre-WWII. The FAA concentrated on the jet operation and left us piston engine pilots to fend for ourselves. No pesky government inspectors rode with us in our sweaty, humid, cramped cockpits surrounded by ancient tube-powered radios that generated ungodly amounts of heat. Flight training for a new co-pilot consisted of three takeoffs, and three landings, accompanied by a day or two of ground school. Frequently, a captain even allowed a pilot-qualified flight engineer to share in the cornucopia of landings bestowed on us by the nature of our short-haul flying. Many captains, within a few years of retirement, chose to bypass the more stressful jet operation. They liked the independence and anonymity of the older fleet. One of our captains—we called him Cuz —had the philosophy that if they couldn't see you, they couldn't find you, so he bypassed operations going directly from his car to the airplane and returned the same way. It is entirely possible everyone except payroll had forgotten him, including the chief pilot, whose responsibility to give him his semi-annual proficiency checks may have been entirely overlooked.

Because of the seniority system, more junior pilots like myself treasured and encouraged pilots like Cuz to continue in their stubborn ways. That meant one less body to climb over on the way to the other division—the one with the jets. I couldn't wait to get into the cockpit of the CV-880. I'd had enough of summer thunderstorms and winter ice, cold fried chicken and lukewarm coffee. Give me those over-the-weather jets with their brewed coffee and rare steaks. Such an innocent I, who had still so much to learn.

Before I could graduate from the division of reciprocating engines, I would be blessed with the opportunity to fly as first officer on our 44-passenger Convair 440 aircraft. This would be my first actual flying position and I looked forward in anticipation to the new adventure. A nasty consequence of this first promotion, however, required that I also remain qualified on the decrepit, graceless and humiliating C-46 freighter we called Dumbo. The only thing the two aircraft had in common were the engines, these being the ubiquitous Pratt & Whitney R2800, 18 cylinder radial engines. There were no passengers, no pretty stewardesses, no hot meals, (no cold meals either) and no coffee except what we brought on board. The Dumbo reminded me of the DC-3 with a bad case of gas, or perhaps more like a giant, over-inflated football than an aircraft. Its size, twice that of the DC-3, leaked rain twice as much. Standard procedure when flying the Dumbo in rain required a pilot wear his raincoat backward, like a hospital gown, so as to stay a little less wet. A roll of standard hardware store silver "duct tape" was part of the cockpit equipment and used to seal the leaky windows in a futile attempt at keeping nature at bay. Training for this aircraft consisted of the obligatory three takeoffs, and three landings, but only four hours of ground school, with most of the time spent trying to figure out the Chinese writing on the control panel, a legacy from the Dumbos' previous owner. Fortunately, I only flew Dumbo on three or four trips. Returning from one of these rare expeditions, Capt. Moldy Sherrill and I were spotted by the chief pilot and called into his office. He looked at Moldy, who stood about 5 feet 6 inches tall, and weighed perhaps 130 lbs., and me, at that time a slim 143 lbs. dripping wet, and declared: "I don't want the two of you to fly the Dumbo together any more because it takes eighty pounds of force to hold the rudder if an engine fails and I don't think the two of you can come up with that much!" While his request may have been in jest, I needed little convincing to avoid being assigned flying duty in the ex Chinese beast. No tears were shed a few months later when one of our Dumbos, landing in a rainstorm, aquaplaned off the runway in Baton Rouge, Louisiana, causing enough damage that the aircraft had to be scrapped.

The CV-440, by comparison, seemed a dream machine, equipped with pressurization, air conditioning, one stewardess and all the respect due a real passenger carrying airliner. The captains were young; mostly Korean War veterans only a few years older than me, a pleasant change from the "old goats" who only wanted to talk about retirement and their ailments. As much as I admired the skill of these senior pilots—and they were incredibly proficient—bantering with someone whose interests more nearly paralleled my own brought a breath of fresh air to the cockpit.

Chief on our minds, of course, is when will the newest jets arrive, and how many pilots would be hired this month. We spoke about career growth, and that equated to advancement, which naturally meant higher pay.

My first flight as co-pilot had me paired with a senior Captain whose reserved personality made the flight uncomfortable and I found myself ill at ease. Nervous anyway, I imagined his disgust at having been paired with a "green" co-pilot with the funny last name and no southern accent. I kept my over active imagination at bay during the initial flight leg from Dallas, Texas to Shreveport, Louisiana. But now it was my turn to fly the aircraft to Baton Rouge.

In 1965, Baton Rouge, although famous as the home of the "Fighting Tigers," Louisiana State University, had zero approach aids to help one find and land at the airport. Complicating my navigation ordeal, there existed a small abandoned military field not far from the main city airport that I did not notice on the aeronautical chart. I didn't notice this airport because I folded my chart exactly at the location on the chart showing the errant airport. With the sky clear and visibility more than 30 miles, I was sure I could spot the "Red Stick" airport without difficulty. In fact, there, right on the nose, an airport appeared. I happily said to my reserved superior, "Captain, I have the airport in sight." He said nothing--and a small warning bell went off in my head. I called for the before landing checklist and began maneuvering the aircraft to position it for an approach to the active runway. I called out "gear down" and the compliant senior pilot lowered the landing gear. The gear had no sooner registered "down and locked" when I realized something had gone seriously wrong. I could not see any runway that matched the magnetic heading of Baton Rouge, home of the "Fighting Tigers." Grabbing my chart, I unfolded it to its full size and frantically scanned it for any airport near Baton Rouge. There, straddling the fold in the chart, appeared a small circle with the name Polk above it and, in parentheses, closed. Oh the embarrassment and humiliation as I turned to my Captain and confessed, "Captain I don't think this is Baton Rouge."

"Son, I think you're right," he said and then added, "Hold your heading and altitude for a few more minutes and you will see Baton Rouge." I humbly did as told and in a few minutes Baton Rouge, home of the "you know what" appeared.

As our passengers deplaned, a middle- aged gentlemen dressed in business attire stuck his head in the cockpit and introduced himself as (I don't remember his name) from the Dallas, Fort Worth Air Carrier Safety Office and proclaimed, "Man, I sure am glad you guys didn't land at Polk Field. It sure would have been embarrassing." Yes sir, I thought, as I slunk down further in my seat, it sure as hell would have been; and without doubt also the end of my brief and glorious career in aviation.

I am happy to report the remainder of my flying over the next three days occurred without incident or embarrassment. I do not know if my quiet Captain had been as momentarily fooled as I, or whether he decided to "teach me a lesson." I decided I had better accept it as a lesson, whether intended or not.

After this first near disaster, my time flying the CV-440 passed without mishap. It did not pass, however, without humor. I recall a memorable flight with Capt. Dave Reno, a noted prankster. I first met him in flight operations while scheduled to fly all night from Dallas to Indianapolis, stopping at almost every airport along the way. After I introduced myself to Reno, he reached in his pocket and pulled out a small box, which at the push of a button popped open, revealing a set of false teeth. The most incredible, infectious laugh then proceeded to emanate from the tiny box in concert with the moving false teeth. I could not contain myself, and neither could anyone else in the room. After he brought everyone near to tears, Reno put the little box away, and we completed our pre-flight duties.

Later that night as we approached Shreveport, La., our first stop, I reached for the microphone to call Shreveport approach control for an approach clearance. Prepared to give ATC (Air Traffic Control) our airline name and flight number, Dave stopped me by raising his hand in a "hold on a minute" gesture. He then pulled out his little laughing box, keyed the mike button, and set off the infectious laughing false teeth. HA HA HA HA HA ... It went on for about ten seconds. I am thinking, "Oh my God, what in the hell is he doing"? And then in a voice as nonchalant as anyone could wish for, came the response, "Good evening, Delta 425, this is Shreveport Approach Control, you are cleared for an ILS approach to runway 13. Contact the tower on 118.7." Dave changed the radio frequency, and repeated his laughing teeth routine and the tower calmly replied: "Roger, Delta 425. You are cleared to land." After landing, communicating only by "laughing teeth," we were directed to our gate. I did not speak a word into the microphone the entire night. Dave had been flying this nightly route so long the entire South and Midwest air traffic control system knew who belonged to the infectious laughing teeth and what it meant. He had all of them superbly trained.

The only break in the routine came on the final leg approaching Indianapolis. Instead of the laughing teeth, he produced a cow that mooed! It worked just as well.

As much as I enjoyed flying the prop aircraft, the itch to get to the jets grew daily. Every day I perused the news bulletins, looking for announcements of new route awards, granted only by the benevolence of politicians. My eagerness had its roots in greed. The first-year salary of $450 per month, and the second-year pay of $600 per month did not leave much left over for luxuries. My 1960 Volkswagen did not have air conditioning, and that made living in Dallas pure hell. Frankly, I had been poor long enough, and lusted after a new Porsche. The vagaries of our union contract dictated that I would get a substantial raise on June 10th

1965. That raise would be even more substantial if I could get a seat in the cockpit of one of our jets. How substantial? Well, almost double my previous salary, because now my pay would be based on a complex combination of airplane speed and gross weight. And as you already know, jets are twice as fast as props! I could smell that new Porsche.

Time and demographics were on my side, but advancement could only come by growth, as few pilots were retiring. The airline industry itself, barely 35 years old, had produced few pilots nearing the age of retirement. But as sure as dawn follows dark, the baby boomers were growing up and going to college. They wanted to fly. Their parents wanted them to fly, and the parents themselves wanted to fly. Everyone wanted to leave on a jet plane and go somewhere. John Denver wrote a popular song about this and "Peter, Paul and Mary" became famous singing that song. As for me, at last awarded a position as a second officer on the CV-880 four-engine jet transport, I too, would be "Leaving On A Jet Plane."

1965: JET JOB

"In order to learn how jets work, I only need to blow up a balloon and let it fly into the air. Somehow this explains it to me."
Quote from an elementary school student of Mark Evans

No more propeller planes! (Or so I thought). I would now be a working crewmember on the fastest, sleekest, most bitchin' (please pardon the colloquialism) jet in the skies, the Convair CV-880. The CV-880 not only looked fast, it actually could fly faster than any other modern jet transport. Designed to fly at 85 percent of the speed of sound, it had four engines, and carried 89 passengers. The pilots sat in seats that looked like they had come out of a Ferrari Formula One racing car. Most transport aircraft pilot seats were more like a kitchen chair with a steering wheel in front. Not the CV-880. You were more horizontal than vertical. Of course I, being only the second officer, had to be satisfied with a seat just like that kitchen chair. None of this mattered because now, as a member of an elite crew on an elite aircraft, my paycheck soared to a staggering $1,000 per month. I immediately ordered a new Porsche. Then, on my first unsupervised flight as second officer, I did something that might cause me to cancel the Porsche, and try to find my old '49 Chevy with the white fender. This is how it happened:

After spending a month learning the intricacies of the CV-880, and a few flights with a flight engineer instructor watching my every move, I celebrated my newly earned promotion by taking a previously scheduled vacation. One week later I returned home on an all-night flight arriving at 6 a.m., aware that my schedule showed reserve duty commencing at 8 a.m. Assuming (wrongly, of course) that I would have eight hours notice of any upcoming duty, I stared in disbelief at the note in my company mailbox notifying me that my first flight as a fully qualified jet second officer departed at 9 a.m. Adrenaline pumping, I raced home, changed into my uniform, and returned to the airport for the 8 a.m. report time. Sleep would have to come later.

Everything went smoothly on the first leg of the day. Capt. Jack Collier, one of the most senior of our line captains, had a reputation as a quiet, patient, but stern disciplinarian and not a back slapping good ol' boy likely to tolerate ineptitude on his flight deck. Frankly terrified I might screw up, I concentrated fully on the job at hand. In spite of my nervousness, the second and third legs went as smoothly as the first, and some of my terror dissipated. As we departed Birmingham, Alabama for New York City, on our fourth and last flight segment, I began to feel a little bit more comfortable. Passing through 27,000 feet, on our way to flight level 350, a giant yawn consumed me and for the first time I felt the lack of sleep. The quietness of the cockpit, with only the gentle noise of air softly whooshing around the windshield had a hypnotizing and sedating effect as my eyelids slowly sank towards the cockpit floor.

"WHAT THE HELL IS WRONG WITH THE ENGINES?" the "quiet" Collier yelled.

Man, did I come awake! I didn't hear anything wrong with the engines but I sure heard his voice. My eyes opened twice the size of the engine instruments staring at me from the flight engineer panel. I did not see anything amiss but I started sweating anyway.

"THEY SOUND ALL OUT OF SYNC!" he roared.

"Er, yes sir, they do," I replied, as my enlarged eyeballs furiously scanned the panel in a desperate attempt to find what had gone awry. In my newly found alertness I also could now hear the engines sounding like four Sunbeam Mixmasters instead of the smooth GE-CJ805, 11,000 lb. thrust-turbo jet engines my company had purchased for their beautiful CV-880 jet transport. My confidence shattered, I imagined my career in ruins. I envisioned tomorrow's newspaper headline reporting that an inept second officer nearly caused a major airline disaster. There would be no new Porsche. I knew I had screwed up, and being too stupid to know what I had done wrong, I threw myself on the mercy of my captain and said: "Captain, I don't know what is wrong, but I am sure it is my fault!"

Now it so happens that Convair, in its wisdom–and to condense everything in as small a space as possible–used a switch to control the fuel tank boost pumps that was not only small, but had a throw of only one-eighth of an inch. Therefore, the positional difference between on and off became almost impossible to recognize without physically moving the switch in the desired direction. I stared at the eight boost-pump switches. (Oh surely I didn't forget to turn them on!) Using eight of my ten fingers I reached for the switches and pushed them all toward the "on" position, all the time praying they would not move (as I would rather the engines all fail and I die a hero then suffer the humiliation of incompetence). But of course they did move. And of course the pumps started up and the engines returned to their former elegant state of harmony and repose.

No words were spoken for what seemed an eternity. Hell, nothing needed to be said. I knew where I stood, and it was in really deep shit. Collier let me drown in it. Soon, however, he turned toward me, and I steeled myself for the coming critique. "Do you remember in ground school how much they emphasized the importance of the boost pumps?"

"Yes, sir, I remember."

109

"Do you remember how they made a big deal out of the fact that the engines would quit above 25,000 feet if you didn't use the boost pumps?"

"Yes sir, I remember that vividly now!"

He said nothing more for a few moments, while I squirmed in my "kitchen chair", sinking further into depression. Then he turned toward me and said: "WELL WE PROVED THE BASTARDS WRONG, DIDN'T WE!"

Thank you Lord for creating men such as Capt. Jack Collier. I got my new Porsche a month later.

The men who captained the aircraft of the 1960s were, for the most part, WWII veterans. They were well educated, and largely of rural upbringing. That so many had been raised on a farm or ranch brought surprise to me as I am a "city boy" and know little of country life. Perhaps this trend of hiring predominantly rural folks existed because the airline I worked for had its roots in the rural South. Perhaps also, because the rural population of this country always had a strong patriotic tradition, and many well educated farm boys were eager to leave their tractor seats for one in the cockpit of a WWII aircraft. In any case, they all had one thing in common, the southern or country accent. Tom Wolfe, in his book, *The Right Stuff*, touches on this phenomenon along with his description of Chuck Yeager, the first man to fly faster than sound. The airline captains of the '60s were contemporaries of Yeager, cut from the same mold. Thus, the image of the "good ole country boy" and his warm, hospitable, and reassuring country voice springs from this culture.

Wherever men gather together for a common purpose, whether a football field, a construction site, a battlefield, or an airline cockpit, they bestow nicknames on each other for deeds or misdeeds. On my airline there is Sky King, noted for his overly rigid cockpit manners and self promoted flying skills, leading one to believe he ranked himself right up there with Lindbergh. Preacher Wells, who always carried a Bible, and would sometimes read and quote from it to his cockpit crew. Scrap Iron Kelly, whose exploits I can only imagine; and Empty Helmet, whose name is self-explanatory.

Sky King, while a no better pilot than any other, just thought he was. His mood swings made him a difficult aircraft commander. He found fault where none existed and lavished praise when unearned. Serving as his co-pilot, you never knew which of your actions would please him or piss him off. This unpleasant character trait made for long, boorish trips, so if your seniority allowed you to avoid flying with him, you did.

I did not personally know Empty Helmet, but at least one story about him is worth repeating. It seems E.H. was a very nervous type, and handled minor emergencies with little grace. Mindful of this, a playful co-pilot decided to increase his stress level by planting a spaghetti-ball of loose wires under the instrument panel in front of the co-pilot seat. Then later, in flight, feigning an instrument problem, the co-pilot assured Empty Helmet that tightening a loose wire would solve the problem. A nervous Empty Helmet exhorted his industrious co-pilot to leave the wires well enough alone until after landing. The confident co-pilot, however, would not be deterred. Reaching under and behind the instrument panel he yanked the wire ball out from under the panel with a victorious shout of: "Voila! I have found the problem!" Empty Helmet went catatonic. Only the realization that he had been tricked saved him from a massive stroke.

Company policy frequently accommodated a junior pilot's wishes if he did not want to be paired with a captain he did not like. Inevitably, however, everyone had to accept an occasional undesirable pairing, and just "grit it out." A pilot who consistently recorded personality conflicts would eventually be called to the chief pilot's office for personality-modification training, commonly known as an ass chewing.

Leadership skills come naturally to some men, while others learn through experience, and watching their more gifted counterparts. A few captains never acquire leadership skills, and instead rely on outdated military stereotypes to guide their actions. This sometimes manifested itself in a "Captain is God" mentality harking back to naval and maritime law. Introduced to civil aviation during the Pan American World Airways flying boat era, this mentality survived long after the flying boats disappeared. One can still find traces of this kind of false leadership in Asian cultures where a junior crewmember is afraid to correct or find fault with his superior. In a modern jet airline cockpit, this does not work, and I will tell you why.

While there can be only one captain in command, and one ultimate decision-maker where the buck must stop, the complexities of a modern jet transport aircraft demand the full attention and skills of all flight-crew personnel. Which, in case you haven't looked lately, usually consists of two, and maybe three pilots for flights as long as 12 hours. An arrogant and demanding captain will find no legion of troops to bail him out in a tight pinch. Instead, he had better find a way to utilize his meager resources in an efficient and timely manner lest he find himself a "chief" in deep doodoo with no "Indians" to shovel him out.

The airline captains of the '60s and '70s still came mostly from the ranks of WWII military transport pilots, but toward the end of the '70s, you encountered increasing numbers of Vietnam fighter jocks. Today, Desert Storm veterans occupy the cockpits and are well trained in the art of sophisticated weaponry and survival under harsh conditions. The military demands courage, and an aggressive nature--as the fighter pilot and his aircraft are necessarily expendable. This is what we expect of our armed forces during a national crisis. The Air Force doesn't train its pilots to help you make your next flight connection.

Unfortunately, the characteristics of a great military pilot–aggressiveness and individuality– do not transfer well into civilian aviation. While you cannot be a Casper Milquetoast and still execute a Category-III blind landing, there are no Distinguished Flying Crosses awarded just because you completed the landing without killing anyone. Surprisingly, neither the airlines nor the military trained their pilots in the essential teamwork skills required to safely operate jet transports in the increasingly crowded civil aviation environment —until a series of tragic accidents underlined the need for such a program. That new program is called Crew Resource Management.

Through most of the 70s, when a captain submitted to his required six-month flight check, it was expected he would fly the airplane and accomplish all the emergency procedures on his own, or from memory, and to order his second in command to accomplish the required procedures. During this era, you were to assume you were alone in the cockpit or at best, with a nitwit for a co-pilot. This reflected the antiquated thinking of the military individualism, and the "Captain as God" culture. Then in the '70s, an Eastern Airline Lockheed TriStar flew into the Florida Everglades, killing all onboard. The probable cause: the entire crew was busy dealing with a minor technical problem, with no one flying the airplane. In 1977, a KLM 747 during take off collided with a Pan Am 747 on a foggy runway in the Canary Islands, resulting in the death of more than 550 passengers. The captain, a very senior management check pilot, made the erroneous decision to take off even though one junior crew-member voiced concern the Pan Am jet had not cleared the runway. Unfortunately, this would not be the last time the "Captain is God" syndrome would kill someone. It did, however, shock the aviation industry into developing new training programs designed to end the carnage.

Crew resource management, or CRM as we call it, taught captains new leadership and management skills. It also demanded a higher proficiency level for first officers. No longer would the co-pilot be thought of as a pilot in training, but rather an essential part of a team effort. Not long after implementation of this program, CRM training would prove valuable when, in 1989, Capt. Al Haines and his fellow crew-members brought a severely damaged and out-of-control DC-10 to a crash landing in Iowa, saving the lives of 162 passengers. In his story, Capt. Haines gives much credit to the superior CRM program developed by his airline.

In my youth, Hollywood depicted pilots as classic heroes. They were tall and handsome, with a little gray hair to lend an aura of maturity and experience. In the 1955 movie, *The High and The Mighty*, I cannot forget John Wayne's swagger as he walks away from the crippled DC-4 he so skillfully flew from the brink of disaster to a safe landing. Or the wise, old mechanic who calls after him: "So long, you ancient pelican!" I get goose bumps every time I recall author Ernest Gann's dramatic story. In truth, however, like professionals in any field, we come in all sizes and shapes. After WWII most airline pilots were former bomber pilots. As a group, bomber pilots were taller than the average pilot. They were assigned to bombers in the first place because they were too damn tall to fit in the tiny cockpit of fighters.

Today, you are as likely to find a 5-foot-5-inch ex-fighter jock piloting your plane, as you are a 6-foot-6-inch B-52 pilot. Nevertheless, there are always the few who, from looks, personality, genetic accident, or good living seem to exemplify the ideal "airline pilot." You will often see one paraded out by their company in newspaper and television advertisements as representative of their flight crew. On my airline, that pilot is Earl Epperson.

While I do not recall that Captain Epperson ever starred in a commercial, he should have.
Earl not only looked the part of "hero airline pilot," he also had the winning personality of a born leader. His athletic good looks, combined with a childlike sense of mischief, endeared him to all

who shared his cockpit. And, of course, Earl fluttered more than a few hearts among the flight attendant corps. As a competent pilot who ran a happy ship, he earned the respect of his fellow crewmembers. This had a positive influence on our passenger service because the cabin crews were delighted to be under his command.

I met Earl early on in my new job as a CV-880 second officer. We were on our way to New York City with stops in Shreveport La., Jackson, Miss., and Birmingham Ala. The "880," an aircraft actually too large to serve smaller cities, operated as a substitute in these valuable markets until a more suitable aircraft like the DC-9 could be put into service. The runway at Shreveport, recently extended to accommodate larger aircraft, still lacked sufficient length to put an "880" pilot at ease. Another problem for my company during this period of exceptional growth, was a dearth of trained flight crews. Therefore, on this particular day, to fill out our necessary crew, we had to dig into the ranks of the DC-6 captains who were previously trained and qualified as CV-880 first officers. The unfortunate pilot assigned that day to serve as second-in-command to the mischievous Capt. Epperson happened to be a former co-conspirator of practical jokes, Capt. Roy Pruitt. Around Earl and Roy, legends grew and myths formed. Their reputation for jokes, pranks, quips, and raillery is renowned. Together, in the same cockpit, only God could know what's in store.

Roy had not flown the "880" in more than two months. Strictly speaking, the FAA found him still qualified to act as second in command on the "880." The rules stated that you must have made three takeoffs and landings in the previous 90 days to be considered "current." The "880" is no docile DC-6, and Roy knew this. Faster than the DC-8 and 707s, and more like a fighter plane than a transport, the 880 is the "hottest" transport aircraft in the sky. In a burst of benevolence Earl said, "Roy, why don't you fly the first couple of legs so you can get the feel for it again." Roy mumbled his consent, but I could detect a lack of enthusiasm

115

because, after all, isn't the Shreveport runway a little marginal for this aircraft?

After takeoff, and with things happening at twice the speed of a DC-6, there is a knock on the door. A flight attendant enters the cockpit carrying a one-year-old baby toting a toy balloon. There were a few courteous "oohs" and "ahs" and "Isn't it cute?" when Earl says, "Hey Roy, is this one of your kids?" Roy responds by staring straight ahead and keeping his mouth shut. His entire concentration is on the short runway only minutes ahead. As the flight attendant departs the cockpit, the child's balloon somehow is left behind. Earl reaches toward the floor, and picks up the balloon, making sure Roy sees that he has it in his hand. Now, let me say right here that Roy is the type of person that, if you sneaked up on him and poked him in the ribs, he would levitate about two feet and let out a stream of obscenities sure to burn the ears off even the least pious among us. Seeing the balloon in Earl's hands, Roy says, "Earl, if you pop that goddamn balloon during my landing you will be forever sorry!"

Earl, feigning hurt, says, "Jeez, Roy, you must be sick, I would never do something like that!" Sitting behind them and listening and watching intently, I am not convinced.

As we approach the runway in Shreveport, I forget about the balloon and concentrate on my duties. Over the approach lights, I look out and see the passenger terminal and the gate agents standing next to portable stairs that will be used to deplane our passengers. The agents enjoy watching the sleek, fast "880" make its landing, knowing full well the short runway will test the pilot's skill. As I lean back in my seat for touchdown I can see Roy's face, tense in concentration, with small beads of perspiration on his forehead.

I cannot say how the balloon popped. I do not see it pop, and I do not see Epperson pop the balloon. Perhaps it is the pressurization, perhaps the balloon is old and it just happened to expire at that moment. I don't know. I just know it popped. And it popped at the worst time imaginable, just as Roy is trying to "slick it on."

Pop went the balloon, and crunch, thud, kerplop went our aircraft. It is not a dangerous landing, just a terrible one. And now Roy lights up, and goes off like the finale of a fourth of July fireworks display. "Earl, you dirty rotten sonofa*%*&*&*%*$$****!"

It is awful.

As we taxi to the gate, the agents are mocking us by holding their hands over their eyes, and pinching their nose. Earl insists he did not pop the balloon, and to show his magnanimity and gracious nature he says, "Roy, I will stand at the door and take the blame, don't worry." (Usually the pilot accomplishing the landing does this so as to accept blame or praise.) This has a mild calming effect on Roy, and even I begin to marvel at our captain's sincerity.

As the passenger door opens and the passengers start down the steps, Earl appears at the cockpit door, and begins to wish everyone a nice day. His voiced is raised just the slightest amount so that Roy can hear his sincerity. "Thank you folks for flying with us today. I sure am sorry about that landing, but you know we have to let the co-pilot land some of the time, or they'll never get any better. We sure are sorry, yessir. You know how it is ... someday he'll learn to land properly, yessir, have a nice day ..." over and over and over, until the last passenger is gone.

The flight attendants adore Earl because his good nature creates a happy atmosphere that rubs off on everyone. It is inevitable that he would attract the attention of more than a few of our female cabin crews. However, Earl is a happily married man with a wonderful wife and family. I never saw or heard anything about his personal life that would cast a cloud on his conduct. Nevertheless, several flight attendants are as good at jokes and pranks as he, and their bantering with him produced some wild stories.

One particular young lady, named Marty, had a running good-natured war with Earl, the origins of which eluded me. When I came upon the battle it had degenerated into stealing and hiding certain articles of clothing essential for personal comfort when away from home. In other words, Earl had taken all of Marty's underwear from her suitcase, and chucked them in a trashcan. This was in retaliation for Marty having strung up Earl's fancy boxer shorts in the first class cabin for all to admire. Marty, on the next trip where they were scheduled together, checks Earl's suitcase to Los Angeles, though their destination is New York! This act became the proverbial final straw. On our next flight together, Earl confessed to me that he had taken drastic action to bring the battle to a conclusion.

Marty had a beautiful new Chevrolet Corvette parked in the underground garage of her high-rise apartment complex. We were all scheduled to fly together that day with a 9 a.m. departure. About 4 a.m., Earl arrived at her underground garage with 50 feet of anchor chain, and several really big padlocks. Wrapping the chain around her rear axle, and then around one of the concrete support pillars, he locks the chain, and leaves her a note that the keys to the locks are on the 10th floor in the fire extinguisher storage box. Marty, thinking it will only take 20 minutes to get to work that morning, finds the note, and races towards the elevator. She rushes to the 10th floor only to find a note in the fire extinguisher box explaining that actually the keys are in the sixth floor fire extinguisher box. Not wanting to waste time with the elevator, Marty runs down to the sixth floor, only to find another note that the keys are in the ground floor fire extinguisher box. Now Earl had timed all this out, and knew how late Marty would be. He explains this to flight operations so they won't call out a reserve flight attendant. In the meantime, Marty still is going floor to floor in her high heels trying to find the damn keys. At last

118

Marty finds the final note that the keys are taped to the underside of the washbasin in the men's rest room on the bottom floor.

When Marty arrives at the airplane about 8 minutes before departure, looking like a wet dog that lost a fight with a cat, she marches directly to the cockpit and says, "I surrender. You win!"

Flying with Earl as his second officer, I watched him closely, studying the way he managed his cockpit and cabin crews. I began to realize flying the line is not just about stick-and-rudder skills. Aircraft were getting larger, and carrying unheard of numbers of passengers. Soon my company would take delivery of the new DC-8-60, a 250-passenger airplane. That is more than three times the number of passengers carried by our largest piston airplane, the DC-7. It is becoming apparent that we would need skills not taught in flight school. But it is still many years before "Crew Resource Management" becomes a reality.

After spending a year on the CV-880, I moved to the larger DC-8, still in my usual second-officer position. I would not be there long, however, as growth took off, so to speak, and advancement came my way.

One day, while taxiing around the perimeter of New York's JFK airport, admiring all the colorful tails on the foreign airliners… it really hit me how badly I wanted to fly to Europe. Had I made a mistake going to work for an airline that seemed mired in perpetual domestic routes? Should I quit this company and try to get hired by Pan American, my all-time first choice of air carriers? It would mean starting all over again, at the bottom of the seniority list. Starting over again would mean years before I could become a first officer, and the likely possibility I would never make it to captain. My emotions were in turmoil. I sought the advice of others, and most said, "Don't even think about it. This airline will someday fly overseas. The politicians can't control it forever." They were oh so right, but at the time I had no inkling of what the future held for me.

My doubts receded as the incredible growth of the airline industry, and my company in particular, created new positions on our newest jets. My seniority now allowed me to move up to a first officer's position on the DC-8, as we continued to take delivery of additional new aircraft. My new position offered the highest pay possible until a position as captain on our new DC-9's became available. Although Douglas aircraft delivered new jets as quickly as they could, my airline needed more. To meet this need, the company purchased a used DC-8 from Pan Am who had decided to standardize their fleet with Boeing 707's. Now, for the first time, but not the last, I will be operating the controls of an international, long range jet belonging to the airline that I had once hoped to be employed by.

Sitting in the cockpit of this former Pan Am aircraft, I imagined myself crossing the Atlantic, on my way to Paris or London. I am shaken from my reverie by Captain Epperson's declaration, "Ippolito, I want you to fly the first leg today so I can study the differences on this airplane." While the cockpit essentially has the same equipment as our own DC'8's, I fail to notice one important difference. As we accelerate down the runway for takeoff, my concentration is fully on the outside, keeping the aircraft aligned with the center of the runway. Earl calls out V1, the speed that demands we continue our takeoff. At his next call out, Vr, I begin to rotate the nose skyward and hold 10 degrees pitch up and await the call of V2, which is the climb speed with an engine failed. As is usually the case, all of our four engines are operating nicely and I must continue to raise the nose lest our speed increase too much. I call for "gear up" and Earl obliges by raising the landing gear. Now my eyes shift from the outside to the instrument panel, specifically to the large airspeed indicator situated just to the left of the artificial horizon. A foreign looking instrument meets my eyes, one with hands rapidly rotating clockwise. It is not an airspeed indicator. Hundreds of hours of instrument flying will not allow me to accept that this is not an airspeed indicator. It has always been there, just to the left of the artificial horizon. I am in a state of panic, my eyes frozen in disbelief. I cry out "Earl, there's no airspeed indicator," as our 320,000 pound jet accelerates to a speed of which I have not the slightest clue.

"It's on the right…on the right side of the artificial horizon."

I force myself to look right. There it is, only inches away from where it is on every other Delta Air Line jet aircraft. It might as well have been located in the passenger cabin, as years of conditioning would not allow my instrument scan to adapt to this new environment. I am grateful we are in visual flight conditions and that our airspeed, in spite of my panic, remains exactly where it should. "How the hell do Pan Am pilots fly like this?" I mumble in discontent.

"Oh, you'll get used to it. That's why I wanted you to fly the first leg."

A few weeks after my crisis, the company modified the former Pan Am cockpit to match the rest of the fleet.

During the years leading up to my being hired by a major airline I became an avid reader of Aviation Week, an industry publication. This weekly magazine, packed with articles about the airline industry, helped me keep abreast of which airline needed pilots. Every so often the magazine published airline accident reports as investigated by the Civil Aeronautics Safety Board. These reports, known as "probable cause" reports, are still published today under the auspices of the National Transportation Safety Board. They are cold, technical and unemotional, with an emphasis on the scientific methods used to determine what went on in the cockpit just before the crash and concluding with their best guess as to the probable cause. No amount of technical jargon, however, can mask the tragedy and sadness inherent in such reporting, and my skin would crawl with goose bumps as I tried to imagine what I would have done in a similar situation.

It is common knowledge that flying as a passenger on a commercial air carrier is safer than driving your car. Nevertheless, when an airplane accident does occur, it is front-page news, and it is little comfort to the passenger to be told that flying is safer than driving. My airline had an enviable safety record when I was hired, and the tragic accidents of other airlines did not touch me personally. It had been four years since my friend Harry Ross disappeared in the mountains of Utah, and eight years since my mentor, Charley Ray, died in his Navion. Now, once again, tragedy would enter my life.

It is 1967, and I am sitting in a DC-8 first officer's seat, reading the pre-start checklist for one of my favorite captains, Jack Lewis, an amiable and competent former WWII B-17 bomber pilot. The boarding agent enters the cockpit and announces the grim news that one of our aircraft has crashed during a training flight. The DC-8 plunged into a hotel near the New Orleans airport killing not only the four pilots on board, but also 10 children vacationing in the hotel. All of the pilots were friends of Jack's, and he cries like a baby. I have never felt so low. Every employee felt somehow responsible. We had done the unthinkable. We had killed innocent children. The entire airline is in mourning, and for months will suffer with shame and guilt.

How had it happened? Our pilots lost control of the DC-8 while practicing landings with two engines throttled back to idle, simulating the loss of two engines. The government requires that a pilot demonstrate his ability to land an aircraft with just 50 percent of the engines operating. This tragic accident, one of several industry-wide training accidents, accelerated the development and use of simulators for pilot training, putting an end to the carnage.

As the 1960s draw to a close, the talk is of larger jets, including a 350-passenger airplane. Already, my company has in service the DC-8-60 series aircraft that can carry up to 250 passengers, the largest passenger-carrying airplane in the world.

The only difference between our standard DC-8 and the "60" series aircraft is the length of the fuselage. It is so similar, in fact, that we need no additional training to fly the "Stretched Eight" as we call it. We can just get in and go. And so this night I find myself in the first officer's seat, approaching New York's Kennedy Airport with Capt. Ray Smith for our first landing in the "Stretched Eight."

Ray Smith is another of my favorite captains. His white hair and warm face complement his mild but firm personality. He flattered me once by asking me whether I thought it a good idea if his daughter married a professional musician. I pondered only a moment before answering, "Probably not." Sadly, as it turned out, I was right, and though the marriage failed, his former son-in-law did not, and went on to some fame as a jazz trumpet player.

With Ray at the controls, we descend toward Kennedy Airport. I notice subtle signs of tension in his demeanor. Because of the aircraft's length, our nose will be considerably higher than the older DC-8 on landing. Pilots understand that the relationship to the ground is a critical factor in whether a landing is a grease job or a disaster. Our eyes watch for this critical position, as there are no instruments sensitive enough to substitute for the eyeball. In the future, sophisticated visual systems will simulate this during training, but in 1968 such systems do not exist. Nevertheless, I have every confidence that Capt. Smith will find the resources to compensate for his lack of experience. About three miles from the runway, and, at his command, I extend the landing gear. His approach technique so far is impeccable, and my confidence in him is strengthened. In fact, I am so confident he will pull off a grease job that, despite his growing consternation, I cannot keep myself from saying: "JUST THINK RAY, YOU'RE FLYING THE WORLD'S LARGEST PASSENGER-CARRYING AIRCRAFT!"

The string of invectives pouring from my commander's mouth directed toward me only heightens his senses and firms his resolve as, sure enough, he slicks it on as pretty as you please, later even

123

drawing compliments from our deplaning passengers. Ray, of course, is most pleased with himself. So pleased in fact, that at our later de-briefing he makes no mention of my verbal prank.

While the DC-8 "stretched" is a big aircraft, there are even larger aircraft being built. Soon Boeing 747s, DC-10s, and Lockheed Tri-Star's will dominate long haul and international flying. There are even plans for a supersonic transport. Once again, I begin to question my choices. Will my airline ever fly these new behemoths? Will I be stuck in domestic service forever? Fortunately, I have little time to dwell on this situation as growth is accelerating and now my time has come. I am awarded a DC-9 captain's position and ordered to Atlanta for training.

56 NORTH, 30 WEST, TIME REMAINING 3:19

"Reliable sources report that mountains have been known to hide out in clouds." Author unknown.

Shanwick Oceanic responds to Gordon's first call and accepts our position report. Again, we are right on flight plan and there are no time adjustments to be made. By some miracle, the HF radio is performing at its best. Keyes takes advantage of our ethereal good fortune, and tunes the backup HF radio to receive the VOLMET weather reports. I am embarrassed to realize I don't know what the acronym VOLMET means, only what it does: provide a continuous broadcast of weather from the European Continent. Keyes finds the proper radio frequencies from a wrinkled, coffee-stained chart called the "Atlantic orientation chart," issued to all pilots but not to flight engineers. Hence, Keyes' chart is a "hand-me-down," discarded by a crewmember as out-of-date. The radio frequencies, however, seldom change, and while Keyes could find this information elsewhere in his books, he is, after all, still a pilot, and prefers using the tools of a pilot.

The weather in Frankfurt is still clear, but we know that upon our arrival this will not be the case. As the temperature and dew point converge with little wind, ground fog will form. After all, it is winter in Northern Europe. Low ceilings and visibility are the norm rather than the exception.

Another flight attendant requests permission to enter the cockpit, but this time she comes armed with a silver tray of fruit and cheese. Keyes sets it on his miniscule desk, and three pairs of eyes peruse the ravaged remains of what was once a first-class culinary masterpiece.

"So how goes it back there?" I ask. She is one of the most senior of the cabin crew, so her salty reply doesn't surprise me. "Most everyone is asleep, except for a couple of assholes with a British rock group who think they are this year's Rolling Stones."

Gordon asks, "Well, did you get their autograph?" She laughs and says, "Well, maybe I should for my teenage daughter."

Inevitably, sooner or later someone famous will board our aircraft as a passenger, and since we are a nation that idolizes celebrities, one is always tempted to seek an autograph or two. Personally, I suppress this urge, as I believe everyone has some right to privacy. Plus, it seems a bit unethical to bother someone who has paid you for a service, expecting to be treated with dignity. I have not, however, been able to always dampen this particular indiscretion.

In 1965, while serving as a very green first officer on our Convair 440 aircraft, I was assigned a route that included stops in the Southern cities of Atlanta, Birmingham and Montgomery, Ala., and Monroe, La. That year, of course, marked the height of the civil rights movement, and the cities on our route were at the epicenter of the demonstrations.

In Atlanta, we boarded Dr. Martin Luther King, and his entourage of civil rights activists. We took them to Montgomery, where they would begin their march to Selma. To say these were tense and volatile times is to understate. I could sense the apprehension of my captain because during that time, airport security as we know it today, did not exist. I must admit that my own emotions were mixed and confused in those days. Yet I sensed that a great man had boarded our aircraft, and I sought, and got his autograph. I cherish it now more than any other I have.

Later in my career, and especially on flights to and from Los Angeles, I frequently saw the likes of Bill Cosby and Robert Culp, along with Andy Devine, who always had two or three nubile young ladies along as escorts. I remember a time when I boarded the aircraft prior to our normal passenger boarding, and became involved in a discussion of personal relationships with a very short, attractive passenger and two flight attendants. Only later did I find out I had been talking to Debbie Reynolds. A similar incident occurred while I traveled as a passenger. After a two-hour discussion with my seatmate on family values, a passenger gave him away when she asked for his autograph. Ironically, soul singer James Brown was accused a few months later of abusing his wife!

In 1983, we boarded a group of passengers calling themselves The Mills Brothers. (I found it hard to believe any of the brothers were still alive.) The flight attendant, of course, had never heard of them, so they offered to sing "It's Only A Paper Moon" to prove they were for real. "There is a catch, however," proclaimed one of the brothers. "You must give us the words to the first chorus." Well, shoot, that is no problem for an old cocktail lounge piano player, so we called their bluff, and damn, they really were the Mills Brothers!

Cheryl Tiegs, Maria Shriver, Spiro Agnew, Frank Blair, and Harry Reasoner were among the many celebrities who trusted their safe passage to my company. But one stands out above all the others.

It is 1965, and I am the second officer on the sleek and fast Convair 880 four-engine jet. We are to depart New York Idlewild (now Kennedy) airport for Houston, Texas. As we board the aircraft, we are told by the gate agent to remain in the cockpit during passenger boarding as the Duke of Windsor (formerly King Edward VIII of Great Britain) and his traveling party have reserved the entire first-class section, and the Duke is not well. He is traveling to Houston for surgery on his eyes, and does not wish to be disturbed. We do as we are told, and on arrival in Houston are directed to a gate that requires stairs to deplane. Red carpet leads from the stairs to the terminal. On both sides of the red carpet, television cameras and press photographers are lined up to capture the arrival of the famous king who abdicated his throne for the love of an American divorcee. "Hey, at least we'll get a glimpse of him as he deplanes," I blurt out in my excitement at seeing a real king. A few minutes later there is a knock on the cockpit door. I open the door to find a tall, elegant, impeccably attired gentlemen who proceeds to announce in the most magnificent king's English, "Excuse me, sir, but I am the Duke of Windsor's secretary, and he wishes to meet the flight crew to thank you for a marvelous flight. May I have your names so I can properly accomplish your introduction?" Bowled over by the correctness of the gentleman's manner, I barely manage to scribble on a piece of paper the names of Capt. Earl Epperson, First Officer Roy Pruitt and myself. A few moments pass, and the former King of England enters the cockpit, and is introduced to us by his secretary. He seems very small, and very ill, but in a gentle, soft voice he says, "Thank you for a very pleasant flight," as he shakes each of our hands. Then he carefully made his way down the stairs, and it seemed a very royal, but sad moment.

I did not ask him for his autograph.

As we approach 20 West, I tell Gordon to roll his seat back and relax, and I will make the call to Shanwick Oceanic.

COMMAND

"The three main crewman on a plane are the pilot, navigator and percolator." Quote from an elementary school student of Mark Evans.

If you were to ask a pilot to name the most important day in his life he might answer, "my first solo flight" or perhaps, "the day I earned my wings" or maybe even "the day my airline hired me." But this is the stuff of youth, and it pales in significance to the victories of adulthood. These youthful triumphs are but stepping-stones along the path of life, doors that open leading to a room, but not the room itself. As the pinned on wings are to the fledgling aviator, so is the fourth stripe to the novice captain. They are but a decoration and it is the command itself that is the cake.

Nonetheless, it is the symbol that draws attention. It is the symbol that demands the respectful glance. For the airline pilot to earn his fourth stripe, he must first apprentice successfully as a second officer, then as a first officer, and then he must be trained, tested, and checked, before he can wear that fourth stripe.

While some have likened an airline captain to the captain of a ship, it is only a cursory similarity. The captain of a ship is in command of a large crew, a crew who does his bidding while the captain oversees and corrects. A ship captain can move from ship to ship, not having to know every intricate mechanical detail of the operation of his vessel as he has an experienced crew to do his bidding. The airline captain, on the other hand, must know every

129

detail of his vessel, and be able to steer and navigate it with precision —for he has but limited crew resources to call upon. The airline captain cannot move from aircraft to aircraft without specific, detailed training on the mechanical aspects of his aircraft. And because the controlling of an aircraft is so much dependent on the visual and tactile senses, he must be given hours and hours of "stick time" – time actually manipulating the controls of his aircraft – so as to hone those senses to a fine point. But in one sense, the ship captain and the airline captain are as one. It is where the buck stops.

Today, in the year 2002, almost all flight training is done in sophisticated simulators that can nearly duplicate the visual and mechanical intricacies of a particular aircraft. If the pilot is fortunate and his company profitable, he may get three or four practice landings in a real airplane during a training flight. Otherwise, it is not unusual to find the first flight on the actual aircraft by a new captain to be a revenue flight. A training captain will act as his first officer and be in actual command. This combination of simulator and on the job training has been proven to be a safe and economical alternative to the old days where training accidents killed too many pilots.

In 1969 few airlines had enough simulators to train their pilots. And even if they did have them, they were not sophisticated enough to properly simulate real-world conditions. Therefore I would learn to fly the DC-9 in the aircraft itself, manipulating the controls in actual flight, subjecting others and myself to the inherent danger of the unskilled. First, however, there must be the inevitable ground school with its emphasis on hydraulics, electrics, pneumatics, heating
and air conditioning, fuel and navigation systems, engine and emergency systems, ad infinitum. Eight hours a day for two weeks. After successfully completing the course, an oral exam is given by an inspector with the Federal Aviation Administration, the overseer of aviation safety. But soon the fun will begin because pilots like to fly their airplanes, not study them.

Jackson, Miss. will be our training base. Why? Because in Jackson, there is a DC-9 that has nothing to do for 6 hours and is therefore available to the student captain in search of his fourth stripe. The DC-9 arrives at 9 p.m. and departs the next morning at 7. That means we will have it from 11 p.m. to 5 a.m. All of our training will be at night, every night, for ten nights.

Jackson, Miss., in 1969, was not exactly a citadel of racial tolerance. While the riots and marches of the early Sixties had ended, tension between blacks and whites did not disappear with the stroke of a pen. And now my company, along with every other U.S. airline, came face to face with the reality of a new era of civil rights. Delta Air Lines sought out and hired its first black pilots. One of the new black pilots, Fred Boone, trained next to me as a first officer.

Fred, a highly intelligent Air Force-trained pilot with a terrific sense of humor, has no illusions regarding his acceptance in the all-white world of airline flying. I have not given much thought to the possible racial tensions we might experience as I am too wrapped up in my own selfish concerns. Besides, as a former musician, I have worked and lived alongside many black musicians, and have not grown up exposed to the culture of the South.

Since Fred and I train together, it is only natural that we spend our few hours of leisure time eating and drinking together. Only while dining at a local downtown Jackson restaurant do I became aware of the sideways glances and snickering remarks aimed in our direction. I find myself coming to Fred's defense by introducing him as a fellow airline pilot. The shocked faces and snide remarks quickly end when Fred speaks, as he has an eloquent and commanding deep voice with perfect diction that says here is a man not to be trifled with.

131

Fred Boone is well aware he is a pioneer, but his self-effacing personality and good humor draw others to him, making him a natural leader. (This served him well in later years, as his ambition drove him into management as a training captain and later as manager of our Lockheed TriStar program.) But for now, poor Fred is just a sorry-ass new hire trying to learn how to fly a DC-9.

Here is how our training is conducted. As a captain trainee, I occupy the left seat with the training pilot in the first officer seat. Other pilots, also scheduled for training, sit in the back, usually in the last row of seats awaiting their "turn in the barrel," and praying they will survive the experience. For six hours, we will fly the aircraft, alternating, with the other pilots waiting their turns. We spend most of our time in the airport traffic pattern practicing normal and single-engine landings. For the new first officers, the training captain will occupy the left, or captain's seat. During Fred's "time in the barrel" he struggles with landings that are less than graceful, until the training captain says: "You know Fred, I think your problem is the natural reluctance of a man of your persuasion to set down in Mississippi!" With the tension eased, Fred's landings quickly improve.

At dinner one evening Fred confessed how much he loved to fly, and how he hoped he would not have to sit around waiting for a first officer position to open or even, God forbid, be furloughed because of a downturn in business. He explained to me with a straight face, how he had called the chief pilot and asked whether in the case of a pilot furlough he could work at the airport as a janitor. Then if the company needed a pilot in an emergency, he could quickly change clothes in the broom closet, and reappear seconds later as "Fred Boone, Super Coon." The nickname will stick with him forever.

On one occasion Fred's sense of humor brought him great embarrassment. A mechanical problem had caused the cancellation of our training aircraft, and we sat around using the time to study. As dinnertime approached several pilots emerged from their adjoining rooms to catch some fresh air, and to ask if anyone wanted to go eat. Fred emerged from the room next to mine, and, looking down the line of hungry pilots, in his most commanding baritone shouted, "Eat, Eat, Eat. Is that all you guys ever think about? Doesn't anybody screw anymore?" The echo of his booming voice still could be heard as a black maid exited the room next to him with a look of shock and dismay. "Shame on you!" she said. "You are supposed to be a credit to your race, an example to others. Go wash your mouth out!" Poor Fred was demolished. But in his defense, I will say that Fred is a credit not only to his race, but also to the human race.

I loved the "Diesel 9", as we affectionately called it. It fit me to a tee. Many transport aircraft have big cockpits where you sit upright with your hands on a massive steering wheel. Not the DC-9. Its cockpit, small and cramped, is exactly the way I like it. I didn't sit in this aircraft, I wore it, thus becoming as one with it. Our early DC-9 models were smaller (shorter) than those that followed, however they were equipped with the engines designed for the larger, longer aircraft. This gave our shorter, lighter aircraft an excess of power that made them a delight to fly. (In later years, the DC-9 evolved from our early 65-passenger models into the MD-90 carrying 148 passengers.) For now, we had a mini-rocket on our hands.

I completed my flight training and easily passed the FAA check ride. (Thirty years later, the fact that I can recall so little of this event indicates how smoothly and uneventfully the whole process played out. This would not always be the case.) Returning home, I agonized over whether to replace my perfectly good three stripe uniform coat with a new coat with four stripes. I decided to remove the three older stripes and have four new ones sewn on. Thrift is sometimes more powerful than ego.

The final step in my training involves flying several revenue flights, acting as captain, but with a training captain babysitting as

133

first officer. During this series of flights, I of course pretend to be in command, but in fact, I am not. A few days later, however, there will be no babysitter.

NOVEMBER 1969

"The Wright brothers are two of the four fathers in aviation."
Quote from an elementary school student of Mark Evans.

I cannot help but revel in my good fortune as I drive to the airport, Dallas's Love Field. Today, I will for the first time be in command of a passenger carrying jet aircraft. I am in the captain's seat barely six-and-a-half years after my hire date, thanks to a booming economy, and the good luck to be employed by a company of sound finances, and exceptional management. I am 32 years old and my logbook records a total flying time of more than 7,000 hours. According to writer and airline pilot Earnest K. Gann, I am at just the right age to assume command. Not too young, but young enough to still possess the small amount of aggressiveness that Gann felt is necessary for the line pilot to complete his mission. Truthfully, however, our passengers preferred captains with a little bit of gray hair, something that would indicate experience and caution. After all, this is not war— it is transportation. For the most part, the traveling public gets its share of gray-headed pilots, as most captains, until now, had spent far more years than I have as second in command. Now, with the drag of the war years gone, the economy is booming and air travel is becoming mass transportation —available to all but the least privileged. And, many other pilots like myself were being advanced to positions of captain. I had not a single gray hair. To make matters worse, I am cursed (or blessed as you may have it) with a baby-faced countenance unable to project much experience and authority. While I brim with confidence, far more than

135

justified, perhaps, I know my appearance might cause consternation among a few passengers.

With a belly full of butterflies, I enter the small room we called operations. With sheer unadulterated pleasure I receive my first greeting of "Good morning, Captain." I reply in kind, and search for the small slip of paper that with my signature will give testimony to my competence in being in command of this flight with its 48 passengers, two flight attendants, and one first officer. Our destination is Shreveport La., a distance of about 200 miles with a flight time of 30 minutes. It might just as well be London, Paris or Timbuktu. I could not be more pleased.

Fortunately, my first officer on this flight, Ron Crispe, is a very experienced pilot graciously aware this will be my first flight in full command. Ron introduces himself, then immediately leaves to board the aircraft so as to complete his pre-flight duties, and perhaps to warn the flight attendants. Meanwhile, I try to make a show out of checking the weather and other pertinent documents, all of which is unnecessary as the weather could not be any better. Then I recall an old saying of my mother's: "God watches over little babies, drunks, and the mentally incompetent." I am counting on this to be so.

I board the DC-9 about thirty minutes before scheduled departure, and Ron and I read through the checklist. As I sit there making small talk with Ron, I notice he is prematurely going bald. Only slightly younger than I, his balding head exaggerates my immature appearance.

Our takeoff and climb to cruise altitude gratefully pass without event when the senior flight attendant enters the cockpit to offer us coffee. She appears a little older than most flight attendants, perhaps as old as 30, and most likely accustomed to flying larger aircraft on longer routes, with crew of more advanced seniority than I. The look of shock on her face speaks volumes about the rapidly changing nature of our airline cockpit crews. "My God," she shouts. "Are we hiring babies? How long have you been flying?" I look at my watch, checking our takeoff time and reply, "About fifteen minutes." She left the cockpit and did not return.

The best part about flying the DC-9, at least for the younger pilots, is the number of takeoffs and landings one has scheduled on any given day. The very nature of the DC-9 is to serve short haul routes, operating in and out of small airports with meager passenger loads. A normal day might include stops at as many as nine airports as we hop, skip, and jump across the South before finally coming to rest. While this can be fatiguing in poor weather, it also hones your instrument-flying skills to a razor's edge. I enjoy making approaches and landings under instrument conditions. It demands the most of my skills. The more complicated the approach, the greater the satisfaction.

Shortly after purchasing Northeast Airlines in 1972, my company began summer service to the islands off Cape Cod. I immediately bid to fly this interesting route as I knew little about the New England area and was anxious to gain experience there. The schedule called for a departure from New York LaGuardia Airport in the morning, proceeding to Hyannis Port, Martha's Vineyard, Nantucket, and a return to LaGuardia, dropping off and picking up passengers along the way. I can think of no other summer vacation paradise with worse weather. Fog can and does suddenly roll in, obscuring the runway. Summer storms and spent tropical depressions blanket the area in gray dripping clouds. The lack of precision approach landing systems at the airports made matters worse. They instead relied on old-fashioned ADF direction finder approaches that made successful landings difficult and hazardous. On one memorable flight we departed New York only to find the weather so poor we could not land at any of the scheduled airports. With 89 passengers on board (our DC-9s were getting longer) we attempted landings at each airport only to be turned away when we could not see the runway at our minimum descent altitude. Three hours later we returned to New York with

89 passengers on their flight to nowhere. This cost my company a lot of money.

I relished the variety of airports and weather conditions offered by the DC-9 operation. Flying from the hot, tropical conditions of south Florida to the ice and snow of New England takes little more than two hours. One evening, leaving Boston and approaching Burlington, Vermont, I received a frantic call from the flight landing just ahead of us. "Don't land," came the cry over the radio. "Go around! The runway is covered with ice, and we damn near went off the end." I immediately did as told. Apparently without anyone noticing, freezing rain had settled on the runway in a matter of minutes. The airport manager sent out for the sanding trucks, and we began a holding pattern while crews laid sand down the full length of the runway. We carefully completed our approach and landing and I drew upon skills I'd learned from a captain with considerable experience in ice and snow. Once on the ground, we could steer the aircraft only with differential thrust. In other words, adding power to the right engine caused the aircraft to turn left, and vice versa. But now we realized we could not stop the DC-9, as even idle power caused the wheels to slide with the brakes set. Using my best guess how far we would slide, I shut down the engines, set the brakes, and slid to a stop about 10 feet from the terminal. Our passengers deplaned via portable stairs, and few made it to the terminal building without slipping at least once. Breathing a big sigh of relief, I called the other crew, and thanked them for saving my ass. He admitted to "not ever wanting to get that close to an accident again."

We weren't finished for the night, so after requesting more sand be laid down on the ramp and runway, we taxied out, and continued on to Bangor, Maine, where on our arrival we found the exact same conditions. No one had bothered to look outside; therefore, no one realized how much ice had formed on the runway and taxiway. Calling on the radio we asked the airport operator to spread sand on the runway, and shortly after, we landed without further problem. However, the airport sand detail had failed to sand the ramp area, and we encountered the same problem with stopping as we had experienced in Burlington. Now, let me say that the ramp in Bangor is something to behold. Having been a former B-52 bomber base, it is about a quarter-mile wide and half-mile long. Knowing I would not be able to accurately position the airplane alongside the modern jet way, I decided to practice my iced-ramp taxiing technique, while they laid down sand near the gate. For about ten minutes I practiced putting the DC-9 into three wheel drifts, and taught myself to recover when I so desired. You will be pleased to know your tax dollars had provided me with the world's largest ice rink to practice my technique. Unfortunately, even with my newly learned skills, I could not safely and accurately position the aircraft next to the jet way, and had to resort to the portable stairs to deplane our passengers some distance from the terminal. I sensed a great sigh of relief from our patient guests.

The reliability of the DC-9 meant few delays or cancellations due to mechanical problems. Only once did we come close to shutting down an engine as a precaution. While holding over Atlanta during inclement weather, I noticed the oil quantity on the right engine decreasing slowly but steadily. Our position as number 10 in the holding pattern meant at least thirty more minutes before we could be cleared out of the holding pattern. A quick calculation showed the remaining oil lasting only ten minutes. Not wanting to risk a single engine approach in low visibility with the possibility of a single engine go around (a dangerous maneuver) I decided we should proceed to our alternate airport where the weather was clear, unless of course, we could land immediately. Strictly speaking, we must declare an emergency to obtain priority handling. At the moment, we did not have one but soon would if we did not land quickly. Advising the controller of our quandary, he quickly and kindly advised, "Delta, you are now number one for approach." After touchdown, we immediately shut down the engine and discovered at the gate that the oil tank had split open, leaving not a drop remaining.

139

HERCULES

"So far planes have only been able to fly in circles of no more then 360 degrees. This could be the next big break-through in air travel." Quote from an elementary school student of Mark Evans.

The economics of the airline industry can be as hard to predict as the path of a summer tornado in Oklahoma. Every downtick in the stock market or upswing in the price of oil is reflected in airline load factors. Americans love to travel, and when they're feeling flush they go somewhere. But when the economy starts to drag, air travel is the first item crossed off the budget. In late 1970, this downturn forced me off my beloved DC-9 and into the cockpit of our newest aircraft, a pure freighter, and civilian version of the famous Lockheed C-130 Hercules. My company called it the L-100, the FAA called it the L-382, the public knew it as the Hercules, and the military pilots called it the Herky Bird. I called it depressing. I felt like a destroyer captain who had been demoted to tug boat driver. All the prestige of my newfound command diminished as I now was in charge of boxes, bugs, frozen fish, fresh flowers, women's wear, and wicker chairs. No more passenger compliments. No more hot coffee served by a pretty stewardess. No more hot in-flight meals. While the DC-9 meals were not all that great they beat hell out of the tuna fish and peanut-butter sandwiches I would be carrying aloft in a brown bag. I was not happy, but not unhappy enough to give up command and return to the first officer seat, so I decided to just grit it out.

The Hercules is a mechanical nightmare. Its four big turboprop engines are powerful, but complex. I had a difficult time understanding the various disaster scenarios emphasized during ground school, so I just memorized everything without really comprehending the minutiae. The aircraft is very easy to fly and land; only the emergency procedures are difficult.

No simulators existed for the Hercules. All our flight training would be in the aircraft, which meant practicing two-engine inoperative landings. No one liked landing an airplane with two engines inoperative. In this situation, all aircraft are difficult to handle, as the two engines "not operating" had to be on the same side of the aircraft, simulating a worse case scenario. Already, there had been far too many crashes in the past 10 years. Too many good pilots and FAA inspectors had died trying to simulate and perfect a crisis that almost never occurred.

During my first training flight on the Hercules, I realized that my instructor seemed not much more comfortable with the aircraft than I was. His nervousness carried over to his instructing technique, resulting in more screaming and yelling than I thought the situation warranted. I kept my mouth shut until the third day when I'd had my fill of his constant invectives and foul language. After our last landing, I said nothing to the instructor, and went immediately to a telephone and asked my chief pilot if there might be another instructor available. While this is the first and only time I'd ever had difficulty with an instructor, in general it was not uncommon, and allowances were made for personality conflicts. The next day a new instructor came aboard whose demeanor and personality turned an ordeal into adventure. As it turned out, the errant instructor with the personality problem decided flight training was not his cup of tea and he returned to flying the line — a task he accomplished in a professional and competent manner.

Almost by definition, the freight operation of a passenger-carrying airline is a stepchild. After all, crates of bananas do not complain, pallets of electronic parts do not require chicken or steak, and it matters little if valuable aircraft engines and spare parts are a few minutes late. Therefore, the attention directed toward our operation came mostly as an afterthought. In some ways this was a blessing, as it lent a casual atmosphere to the entire enterprise. The down side, however, showed itself as a lack of attention to maintenance. Passenger flights came first; frozen fish could wait.

After completing flight training and flying several revenue flights, I still hadn't gotten over my uneasiness about the complexity of the propeller emergency procedures. There were too many complicated actions for the many possible disasters and I felt overwhelmed. If a mechanical failure of the propeller occurred, one is expected to weigh all of the possible alternatives and make the proper decision within seconds. I had little confidence in my ability to accomplish this rapid fire type of decision making--and then of course, my worst fears came true.

We had no more than lifted off the ground in Atlanta, bound for New Orleans, when the number-one engine failed. My mind raced, and could come to no other conclusion but to do what I had done those many years flying piston-engine airplanes, and that is to call for the throttle back to idle, fuel to be shutoff and the propeller to be feathered. We did not fall out of the sky. In fact, hardly anything occurred except that engine winding down to a stop as we continued around the airport, and landed without further ado. I still felt uneasy, however, and could not squelch the notion we had just gotten lucky. Two weeks later, as we were approaching New Orleans airport in a different aircraft of the same type, the number-four engine suddenly started to surge with the RPM crazily going up and down. The sound matched the noise a small boy would make with a model airplane in his hand, pretending to be the Red Baron. Again, I could not recall if this is covered in page two, paragraph six, or perhaps one of the exceptions that proves the rule, or is it scenario number ... and, in disgust, I said, "Fuck it, just feather it."

143

That I am here to write about this should tell you not much happened, and we landed normally and that should be the end of it … but not quite.

A few weeks later a fellow pilot attending the C-130 ground school approached me. Introducing himself, he said, "Captain, I am having trouble understanding the prop emergency procedures, and the FAA inspector said you are the 'expert' with more propeller failures than anyone else." Stunned into near apoplexy, I said, "You tell Mr. Newman (his unforgettable name really is Paul Newman, no relation of course to the actor) that is the most absurd assumption I have ever heard!" Then, thinking better of it, I said, "Perhaps you shouldn't tell him anything —just do the best you can." I quickly left the confused student before he could start asking questions I couldn't answer.

The loose operation of the freight division allowed us a few liberties not available to our human-bearing brethren. For instance, a few pilots loaded their motorcycles onboard to use on long San Francisco layovers. Pieces of furniture were transported to distant relatives. I, for one, decided to buy a small English sports car, and had it loaded onboard in Newark for transport to Dallas. My luck ran out, however, when a mechanical problem caused us to abort the flight in Atlanta, before reaching Dallas. There it sat in all its glory, waiting for available space to complete its journey, when an admiring senior vice president noticed the address on the fender, which bore my name, rank, and "comat" tag (company lingo for free transportation). While my company allowed small packages to be shipped via company mail, a whole automobile pushed the limits of tolerance. With my tail between my legs, I towed a trailer to Atlanta, and retrieved my precious cargo before they socked me with an $800 freight bill. A few days later my company posted a notice to employees that ended forever our clandestine personal freight operation. What miniscule esteem I might have enjoyed among my fellow pilots had now been dissipated.

144

As the type of cargo we carried could be as varied as all humanity itself, it was not uncommon to be loaded with 1,000 pounds of Lady bugs from California destined for the rose growers in Tyler, Texas, or thousands of newly hatched chickens destined for some Arkansas chicken farm. Municipal zoos used our aircraft to transport live, wild animals from one to another.

On one memorable flight we were loaded down with an incredible number of baby chicks, and a couple of sedated lion cubs. We usually flew overnight, and on occasion would strike up a conversation with the air traffic controllers, there being no one else in the sky at that time of night. One controller asked how we liked the freight operation, and did we miss having a few pretty stewardesses on board. I replied, "Heck no, this airplane is loaded down with chicks and wild pussies!" His silence was deafening, until I told him about our cargo. "Thank you for explaining," he finally replied.

In 1971, my company took delivery of additional DC-9s, and I got my old job back. The freight operation had its good moments, but I was happy to be flying people again.

1972

"It is always better to be down here wishing you were up there, than up there wishing you were down here." *Author unknown*

I like Christmas. I especially liked working during the Christmas season. Surely for some people the holiday season is a time of stress. For the passenger, the holidays mean no bargain fares, frequent flyer miles that are impossible to use, crowded airplanes and airports, and for much of the Northern Hemisphere, bad weather. Still, it is one of the unique times of year when people constantly are reminded to be of good cheer, and to love their fellow man. This actually works! Christmas travelers usually are with good cheer. After all, most are traveling to visit loved ones —on purpose. It is a time when leaving on a jet plane makes possible the nearly impossible. The joining of families separated by thousands of miles can, in fact, be accomplished in a few hours time.

The abundance of good will generated by the Christmas spirit often is tested by winter weather, however. After December 15, few northern cities either in the United States or Europe escape the wrath of Mother Nature. Yet even this is welcomed by most. Don't many of us dream of a "White Christmas?" Thus, in the winter of 1972, a storm of monstrous proportions struck the northeastern seaboard of the United States.

It is also the winter my company bought and merged with Northeast Airlines, an airline whose primary customer base and routes covered this region. When one airline buys another, problems always crop up regarding incompatible equipment. One memorable and comical example of this occurred with our discovery on departure from Ft Lauderdale, Fla., to Boston that our airplane came equipped with food ovens having only the capability to keep a pre-cooked meal at serving temperature. Unfortunately, the meals on board were frozen solid. Someone had mistakenly assumed that all Delta aircraft had the special high-temperature ovens necessary to cook these frozen meals. Still, the Christmas spirit prevailed, and few complained when they were offered a choice by the flight attendant of "Drink or starve?" Few chose starve. And few were fit to drive home on arrival in Boston. I trust they were met by loving relatives.

A much larger problem before us, however, was the weather. On December 23rd, the snow had stopped, but many smaller New England communities were buried under snowdrifts as high as twenty-five feet, and so were their airports. The Currier and Ives panorama put our operations managers to the test. Making matters worse, few of us had any experience flying into and out of such heavily snow-impacted areas. Most of our flying had been through cities south of Boston. Our new Northeastern brethren were supposed to do most of the flying into the smaller New England cities, as they were highly experienced in that region. Unfortunately, our aircraft were not compatible, meaning they could not fly ours, and we could not fly theirs due to dissimilar instrumentation.

And so it is on this day, December 23, 1972, we have the only DC-9 in Boston with operating rear air stair doors (steps extending from the tail). The city of Presque Isle, Maine, has been snowed in for 10 days with no flights in or out of their airport. While the airport operator had managed that morning to plow the runway clear, the passenger steps normally used to deplane passengers are buried under twenty-five feet of snow. Ours being the only suitable aircraft available, we are assigned the task of flying in and taking out eighty-nine passengers on the verge of losing their Christmas good cheer.

I confer with the captain whose DC-9 is unable to accomplish its former mission and seek his advice. He happily obliges, as now he will head for Florida in my place. "What you gotta do is after you land, you must stop before you get to the only place possible to turn around. If you pass it up, you will be stuck there for days, as the snow on each side of the runway is piled up over ten-feet high, and your wings will not clear the snow banks. They plow a special turning place for you about one-third of the way down the runway. This lets you turn around and taxi back to the terminal area, which is a little shack about twenty-by-twenty feet located at the landing end of the runway. The company man has a radio so you can talk to him directly when you get there. There is no control tower. The only approach navigation aid is the VOR but it looks like visibility is good up north this morning, so you shouldn't have any trouble finding it."

Armed with this condensed version of our mentor's years of experience, we leave Boston for Presque Isle, where the weather is very clear, with more than twenty-five miles visibility. However, with wind blowing from the northwest at 35 knots, and a recorded temperature of -18 degrees Fahrenheit, calling this "good weather" seems overly buoyant. No one found it necessary to compute the wind chill factor.

As we approach Presque Isle, I am impressed with the near Arctic look of the terrain that, until then, I had only read about. The depth of the snow covers almost every identifying feature, with the snow-white panorama in contrast to the cobalt blue sky. The sun, directly overhead, casts no shadows from the few trees poking above the snow. Mother Nature has made her bed this morning with an immense cotton sheet covering northern Maine.

According to our approach chart we will fly a northerly leading from the VOR to the 4.2 mile-DME fix (distance

149

measuring equipment). This will put us about one mile from the end of the runway, where we should be in landing configuration, and 400 feet above the ground. With our landing gear down, and our flaps set, we begin the descent after passing the VOR. I can see nothing but white before us; however, I am confident as we near the 4.2-mile fix we will see the airport. I could not have been more mistaken. The closer we get, the wider my eyes open, until at the 4.2-mile fix I turn to my first officer and say, "Have I gone blind? I don't see anything but snow out there?"

He hesitates momentarily, and then with resignation says, "Jesus, I don't either." It is as if Presque Isle Airport has been plucked off the face of the earth. My mind races to think what we might have done wrong. I halfway expect to hear the Twilight Zone theme song in the background when instead over the radio, there is a shout.

"I see you, you are almost right on top of us." The company man in Presque Isle is calling us on the radio. "Now you're right over me."

I bank the plane steeply to the left to see what I can see. And there, 400 feet below us is a barely visible furrow. Drifting snow has obscured the dark pavement of the runway. With the sun directly overhead, not even the 10-foot snow banks on either side of the runway cast a shadow. At the landing end of the runway I can see a solitary figure in navy blue, standing on the roof of a shack, waving frantically at the first airplane he has seen in 10 days. I swear I can hear him say, "Please come back and land," but perhaps I just imagine it.

Barely able to keep the nearly invisible runway in sight, I make a very tight approach and land, following the sage's advice about stopping and turning around. We get a nice round of applause from our ecstatic deplaning passengers, and another round of applause from our newly boarded—and equally ecstatic—passengers when we later depart.

150

From November 1969 to February 1975, I estimate having made more than three thousand takeoffs and landings. From the frozen forests of Maine to the scorched desert of Arizona and in between, there are few commercial airports I have not visited in my trustworthy, reliable DC-9.   From the standpoint of sheer flying pleasure, one could not ask for better duty.

TRAINED TO DEATH

"Lovers of air travel find it exhilarating to hang poised between the illusion of immortality and the fact of death."---Alexander Chase, "Perspectives, 1966"

In the course of everyday life, trying to make some sense out of tragedy is difficult. In the aviation field, it is not only difficult, but also mandatory. The number of training accidents in the airline industry had become epidemic, and the loss of human life a blight on the integrity of the aviation community. In 1972, a close friend, Frank Cook, two of his colleagues, and an FAA operations inspector were killed in what at first was an inexplicable accident while learning to fly the DC-9.

As our company's DC-9 approached the runway, a DC-10 "wide body" (an aircraft wide enough to have two passenger aisles) operated by another airline, had landed and immediately taken off in what is called a touch and go landing. Crossing the runway threshold just as the DC-10 lifted off, the DC-9 rocked back and forth, and finally rolled over on its back and crashed on the runway, killing Frank and three other pilots on board. Aircraft wake turbulence appeared the likely cause. In 1972, wake turbulence seemed a trivial matter of little danger to the aviation community. This accident forced a re-evaluation of the little understood phenomenon that seemed to appear in the vicinity of the new wide body "Jumbo Jets." The National Transportation Safety Board (NTSB) and NASA launched a major research program. Months of wind tunnel and low-level flight-tests using smoke generators eventually revealed the existence of invisible and deadly wing-tip vortices.

This mini-tornado-like wind streamed back from the wingtips of very large aircraft like the DC-10, Boeing 747, and the Lockheed TriStar. In calm wind conditions, the vortices posed grave danger to landing aircraft, and, in fact, were the cause of the deadly crash that claimed Frank and his colleagues. Investigators determined that for the vortex to dissipate sufficiently, landing aircraft needed a five-mile separation between any aircraft and any "wide body" aircraft. This separation is one of the reasons it is so difficult to increase the rate of takeoffs and landings at our crowded airports.

About this time, simulators with sophisticated visual systems began to arrive in the training departments of every major airline. Computerized images of the real world, as viewed through the cockpit window, allowed the airlines to practice dangerous maneuvers such as two-engine inoperative emergency landings without killing off their trainees. As computer technology advanced, these images became so real it became possible to simulate the runway and taxiways, including the terminal building of any airport in the world. Training accidents, and their inevitable loss of life, would become a thing of the past. Meanwhile, we pilots received far better training at far less cost, than could be accomplished in the actual aircraft.

Frankly, simulation-training sessions actually could be fun, and allowed us to do things we could not possibly do in the actual airplane. For instance, one favorite simulated stunt had us flying across the airport at 400 mph, and attempting to fly through the company maintenance hanger. If the doors were closed, it didn't matter. Having successfully pulled off this maneuver, (few did without causing a simulated crash) one could then pull up and do a barrel roll. Another important training maneuver simulated an aborted landing because of another aircraft or perhaps a truck or cow on the runway. We killed a few cows and smashed a few trucks, sometimes on purpose, all, of course, simulated, but the fun was real.

By 1975, my airline had tripled in size through growth and mergers. The number of pilots nearing retirement increased and my seniority now entitled me to fly the Boeing 727, a larger aircraft than the DC-9, offering a better paycheck. My company, now equipped with the latest wide body aircraft, including the Lockheed TriStar, the DC-10, and the Boeing 747, offered a promising and bright future, except in one area: international flying.

I don't know why my passion to fly over water to distant and foreign countries is so strong. Perhaps it comes from the tales I read, as a schoolboy, of the fascinating voyages of Sir Francis Drake, Ferdinand Magellan and Captain Cook. My wanderlust needs to discover distant lands, even though others have long ago discovered them. I would as soon stare at a map as order dinner from a menu. A navigation chart becomes a work of art, promising a path to romance, adventure, discovery, and possibly danger. The desire to know what is on the other side of that hill, that mountain or that ocean, is as dear to me as the beat of my heart.

Oh how I envied the pilots of Pan Am and TWA, for they could cross oceans, and I could not. It seemed so unfair that only two airlines flying the U.S. flag held the power to transport its citizens to Europe. Were I not so consumed with my own disappointment, I might have noticed that the political winds were beginning to shift. And, I might also have noticed the misery of my fellow pilots at Pan Am and TWA as their companies, mired in debt, began to sink in profitability while my company's earnings soared higher.

In February 1975, after six weeks of ground and flight training, I became rated in the Boeing 727, and began revenue line operations. My company now had a flight simulator with the latest visual system, and I completed most of my flight training in this complex computerized box. Just past my 38th birthday, I was now in command of a crew of three pilots and four flight attendants.

The second officer seat on the Boeing 727 is an entry-level position with my company; therefore the pilot occupying that seat is usually the youngest. The passing years had put a few lines of age on me, and I no longer had the "baby face" of years past. This actually came as a relief, as I grew weary of the references to "Captain Kid." It pleased me even more when one evening, after the passengers had been served their meals, the 40-ish senior flight attendant entered the cockpit, and announced: "There are only two meals left over; one for the captain, and one for the co-pilot." With a flirtatious wink at the young second officer she said: "YOU WILL BE BREAST FED!"

In recalling the old saying familiar to all involved in aviation that "flying is hours and hours of boredom, punctuated with moments of stark terror", I am grateful to report those moments of stark terror are less and less frequent, thanks to the jet airplane and modern technology. However, the hours and hours of boredom, for the line pilot, sometimes can stretch into weeks and even months. Frankly, this is exactly what aviation has been trying to achieve, and what most passengers are quite happy to live with. Passengers, of course, now can pass the time with sophisticated in-flight entertainment systems, magazines, playing cards, and telephones. Even laptop computers now help pass the few hours that one must spend confined in an ever-shrinking passenger cabin.

For flight crews, the relief from tedium often takes the form of humor. They put the movies behind us, so we can't see them; therefore we are left to our own devices when things get too humdrum. This situation existed for me in the winter of 1975 — plodding back and forth between Dallas / Ft.Worth and Denver, over uninteresting terrain, in perfect weather, with absolutely nothing amiss, week after week. Just what our passenger's want, I thought, but frankly for me, I was bored.

Staring out the cockpit side window at the bleak landscape below, I began to recall my youthful days playing the piano at Charley Ray's nightclub. Charley had the unique ability to make up stories on the spot that somehow would relate to his audience, and that of course kept them coming back for more. I had learned a little of his technique, and a mischievous plot began to form in my benumbed brain.

On board our flight that day, we had a fun-loving, prank-playing flight attendant whom the passengers absolutely adored, showing their appreciation with blizzards of favorable letters. Our good-natured flight attendant is not above pulling a prank or two on the cockpit crew, thereby inviting retaliation. On that very morning, in fact, the first officer—in dire need of a cup of coffee—had slipped a note under the cockpit door that led to the forward galley. On it he wrote: "Help, we are being held hostage, please send coffee!" A few moments later a large piece of paper well stained with fresh coffee appeared from under the door, into the cockpit. Such blatant good humor did not go unpunished.

As we passed abeam a non-descript village somewhere in the wastelands of eastern Colorado, I began a public address announcement to our passengers, who did not yet have the benefit of in-flight movies. "Ladies and Gentlemen, this is the captain speaking, and I am pleased to announce that we have on board today's flight last year's Queen of the Apple Core Annie Petrified Apple Core Festival. The little town you see off our left is Apple Valley, Colorado, where the festival is held." (Of course this is not the name of the little non-descript village.) "As legend would have it, it seems that sometime around 1874 one of the early pioneers, a woman named Annie, decided to settle in this area, and plant the many apple cores she had saved during her long covered-wagon journey, in hopes of starting an apple tree farm. She, of course, became known as Apple Core Annie. Unfortunately, drought and pestilence caused her apple cores to petrify, and no apple trees ever grew. This was thought to be just a legend until recently a farmer dug up these petrified apple cores, and, being a member of the

157

local Chamber of Commerce, he decided to promote an Apple Core Annie Petrified Apple Core Festival, and naturally select a Queen for the Apple Core Annie Petrified Apple Core Festival. So when you see the tall, attractive blonde in the passenger cabin, just say, "Hello Miss Queen of the Apple Core Annie Petrified Apple Core Festival." And if you find that a mouthful, you can address her as we do. We just lovingly call her 'HARDCORE.'"

Hanging up the PA microphone, I notice the humorless first officer has an incredulous look on his face. Had I gone too far? No, the second officer is laughing his ass off. Still, I began to think I might have overstepped the bounds of decency, as there is no reaction from the cabin crew. Then came a loud knock on the cockpit door. The second officer opened the door, and there, in all her glory, stood our tall blond attractive prankster. On her lovely head, cut from a paper ice bucket, sat a crown, fit for a queen, while across her chest she had pinned a banner made from a first-class tablecloth, proudly exclaiming "MISS HARDCORE 1973." She wore it the rest of the day.

56 NORTH 20 WEST, TIME REMAINING 2:37

"Kitty Hawk was the first female pilot." ---Elementary school student

With the still-cooperating HF radio, I complete our position report to Shanwick Oceanic, and am given instructions to call Scottish Control at 56 North, 10 West. Gordon has left the cockpit for a stretch, so I don the my oxygen mask. Wearing the oxygen mask at high altitudes when one is alone at the controls is good practice. It is also mandatory. Woe to the pilot who forgets this when a government inspector is on board, for he will pay the price with suspension.

Gordon returns to the cockpit, and puts on his mask, while I untangle myself from earphone and oxygen lines, and exit my seat. We have been aloft more than eight hours. My butt is sore, and my legs cramped. For a moment, I have empathy with economy class, but at least I have a view.

The passenger cabin is almost totally dark as I leave the cockpit. Sprinkled randomly among the seats is the occasional beam of reading light. As I walk slowly down the passenger aisle, I attempt to avoid, with little success, the many feet projecting from the cramped economy seats. A chorus of "oops," "sorry," and "ouch" follows my path to the rear of the aircraft where I find several flight attendants hovered over the food carts preparing to serve breakfast.

Kenda is among them, and she greets me with a friendly, "Well, the old man finally comes out of his hole. How ya doin?" We make small talk for a few minutes, and then she asks, "Do you think they will put the ER on this flight?"

She is referring to the Boeing 767 "extended range wide body airplane" rapidly replacing the Lockheed TriStar, and DC-10 aircraft on international routes. I reply that I didn't think so because the B 767, while a newer aircraft, is just a little bit slower than the Lockheed TriStar, and could not fly the Los Angeles to Frankfurt route in less than twelve hours on a regular basis. Kenda seems perplexed at my answer, so I try to explain the arcane world of Federal Aviation Administration crew flight time limitations.

"It seems our government feels two pilots and a flight engineer do not get as tired as just two pilots. Therefore, a TriStar can be scheduled for up to twelve hours of flying, whereas a Boeing 767 two-pilot crew can only fly for eight hours. If the flight is more than eight hours, a Boeing 767 must have a third pilot on board. This is so that one of the pilots can actually rest or sleep during the twelve-hour flight. Apparently, the government feels that pilots who operate airplanes that require more than two cockpit crewmembers are somehow able to stay awake longer than pilots who fly airplanes that require only two cockpit crewmembers. Therefore, the Boeing 767 would require four cockpit crew-members with at least two captains in order to exceed twelve hours flight time. Hence, the extra crew member expense negates the lower operating cost of the Boeing 767 ER, therefore the answer to the question is no."

Kenda's glazed eyes look directly into mine, as she says, "Get the hell out of my galley and go back to work!"

I comply with her order.

As I return to the safety of the cockpit, Keyes remarks that my tour of the passenger cabin seemed brief. "Yes," I reply. "I was thrown out."

COMPETITION COMES TO THE NORTH ATLANTIC

"This is a nasty rotten business."----Robert L. Crandall, CEO, American Airlines

In the incubating days of the aviation industry, political connections had more to do with future success than any effort put forth by its employees. The airline pilot who chose to work for a particular company because of its prestige or regional desirability might find his career in ruins because of government capriciousness. On the other hand, the pilot who took the first job available often found that luck and good fortune placed him under the benevolent hand of friendly bureaucrats, and his days are spent in glory and remuneration. Aware of this in only the most primitive way when I joined my company, I watched in amazement as fate and fortune shined favorably on my company while my brethren with other airlines suffered the agony of forced mergers, buyouts, and bankruptcy.

To the airline pilot, the seniority system is the quintessential element of life. It is the final arbiter of when and where he will sleep, when and where he will fly, how much he will earn and when he will vacation. It is more than a mere number on a list. It is the ultimate pecking order. Once a pilot is judged competent to occupy a flight crew seat, it is seniority alone that governs promotion — subject, of course, to the fortunes of his employer. For the company lacking good fortune and profits, a merger with a more prosperous air carrier is often its savior. The ensuing battle over seniority can cause chaos, bitterness and retribution. My company, with its abundance of good fortune, found itself on three occasions as mediator of these seniority battles when we bought unprofitable companies on the brink of bankruptcy. It mattered not that the merged company became more than the sum of its new parts, and all would be far better off in less time than could be imagined. For some, it was humiliating, a stripping of prestige, and they would carry their anger for years. Thankfully they were few, for the majority could see the benefits of consolidation.

When I first heard the word "deregulation" I grew apprehensive. Although airline pilots are fiercely independent individuals, we work in an industry where cradle to grave loyalty is the norm rather than the exception. Our industry was nursed to maturity by government largesse, mainly through subsidies for carrying the mail. Perhaps you are too young to remember how everyone had to pay extra to send a letter "air mail." (An airmail stamp in 1932 cost 24 cents.) The airlines of the U.S.A. received this airmail surcharge to cover the expense of carrying the mail and any excess was used to cover any other expense they needed to stay in business. If an airline lost money, then a fare increase would be approved or a new profitable route would be granted, insuring the airline would avoid bankruptcy. No one could start an airline unless the Civil Aeronautics Board approved it. In fact, after WWII, only a few small, regional "feeder and cargo airlines" were allowed to begin service as long as they did not compete with the "Big Five," as United, American, TWA, Eastern, and Pan American were called. The others, Delta, Continental, Western, Braniff, National, and Northeast were brushed off as "regional trunk carriers" with little relevance to the national scene. Only two airlines of U.S. registry, TWA and Pan American, were allowed to carry passengers over the emerging North Atlantic and Pacific routes to Europe and Asia. Routes from the continental U.S. to Hawaii were awarded as political spoils. Nonstop service from the winter-bound Northeast to the balmy Florida peninsula was granted those who provided generous financial and political support to the incumbent government. Then in the late 1970s,

Alfred Kahn, an economics professor and head of the Civil Aeronautics Board declared, "Enough is enough! Let there be competition!"

The announcement in 1978 that my company will be awarded a route from Atlanta to London brings me boundless joy. No longer will my company be landlocked. No longer will the ocean be an impregnable border. Of course, it is only one route, once a day, seven days a week. It will require eight captains, eight first officers, and eight second officers to fly our leased L-1011–200 international aircraft to the limit of its range and payload. Alas, I have nowhere near the seniority to hold a captain's position on this prestigious route. Although I have now been on the property for more than 15 years, I am still hundreds of numbers away from a position on our new wide-body aircraft. I can, however, bid back to co-pilot or first officer status.

It is difficult when one has attained command to return to a subordinate position, but my desire to cross an ocean is of such intensity that I swallow my pride, and enter my bid as second in command. Somewhere in the back of my mind is the thought, "I may never get the opportunity again to fly the Atlantic. Don't pass this up." Five others, more senior than me, with a desire as intense as mine, are awarded positions ahead of me. Nevertheless, the sixth position is mine. Now I am faced with the misery of three weeks of ground school, and the delight of two weeks of flight training. I bear this cross by reminding myself everyday where I will go when it is all over.

I am scheduled, as the first officer, to fly the second flight my airline will operate to London. Naturally, I would have preferred to be on the first, but I resign myself to the second. Besides, the first flight will be manned with management pilots, baby-sitting the regular line pilots who will fly the route on a regular basis. What a laugh this seems. The baby sitters know no more than the babies they are sitting! My company is the first "virgin Atlantic" airline, with all due respect to Richard Branson, and his present-day Virgin

Atlantic Airline. Atlantic Ocean flying has been an elite and exclusive club due to the monopoly routes of TWA and Pan American. They controlled the entire expertise from their offices on the east and west coasts. No one in land-locked Atlanta knew how in hell to fly the North Atlantic, as up till now, all ocean flights have originated from coastal cities. TWA and Pan American are not eager to share their wealth of experience with the neophyte international airlines operating from inland cities. They recognize the danger we pose to their existence, which turns out to be all too real. My company, in a desperate search for knowledge, sends one of our pilots on Air Canada to London to learn the unfamiliar and complex North Atlantic procedures. Upon returning, he passes this knowledge on to us in a one-day "International Procedures School."

Feeling shortchanged and unprepared for this new endeavor, I peruse every map and manual I can get my hands on. I am determined not to be embarrassed. After all, we are very experienced pilots. How different can it be flying over water instead of land? It will be very different, as I will soon find out.

The inaugural trans-Atlantic flight goes off without a hitch. I feel relieved and proud, but now it is my turn to perform in an informed and professional manner. In other words, I do not want to screw up.

Good fortune is with me as I am scheduled to fly with Capt. Charley Green, a very senior pilot, and former flight-training instructor, whom I remember from my DC-6 flight engineer days fifteen years ago. Charley inspires confidence, and our departure from Atlanta proceeds without incident and on time. My first inkling this will not be an ordinary flight arrives as we cross the U.S.-Canadian border and are queried by Montreal Center, "Hey Delta, where are you guys going? Don't you want a descent into Montreal?"

Charley is at the controls so I pick up the mike to reply. I can hardly contain myself as I answer as nonchalantly as I can, "No sir, we are going to London, England." There is a moment of stunned silence. After all, this is as new to him as to us. U.S. aircraft did not fly from inland cities to Europe.

In a tone of disbelief, Montreal Center asks: "Is this a charter flight?"

"No sir," I reply. "This is a regular, scheduled passenger flight from Atlanta, Georgia, to London, England."

"You mean you're going to do this every day?" he asks.

"Yes sir, every day," I answer. I so badly want to add: Every day of every month of every year until the day I retire. We are now an honest-to-God United States international flag carrier.

"Well, good luck, and have a nice flight. I will let the others here know this will be a regular daily flight in the future."

"Thank you," I reply, trying to keep the buttons on my shirt from bursting as my heart swells with pride.

Shortly after my conversation with Montreal, I stumble through the procedure to obtain our oceanic clearance. So far, so good, but a knot grows in my gut as we enter the North Atlantic Ocean east of Newfoundland. Not because we are entering a new and unfamiliar environment, but because soon I will have to make my first oceanic position report on HF radio, and everyone including God, will be listening. I do not wish to look the fool.

I listen intently to others ahead of our flight. Their transmissions are smooth and faultless; full of confidence and experience. Out of respect for their special status, they are granted call signs that further add to their mystique and infallibility: "Speedbird" for British Airways; "Clipper" for Pan American, while my company is relegated to being called by its international bag tag identifier, Delta Lima, the phonetic spelling for DL. It is as if we are crashing an elite party at an exclusive resort. Nevertheless, not sure if I should be ashamed, embarrassed or just plain mad, I make my call. It is not faultless, it is not smooth, but it is accurate. Yes, I did get a few comments over the common frequency, such as, "Hey, what are you guys doing over here? I thought you couldn't fly over water!" We can, and we are. And on a subsequent trip, showing a little more self-confidence, I even take the oceanic controllers to task, and tell them to kindly use our corporate name when they call, and drop the Lima nonsense. They accept our request, and by the early 1990s, if there are any elite and exclusive parties to be given in the international arena, my company will be doing the inviting.

For six months I served as first officer on our sole trans-Atlantic flight, making weekly crossings to London. My company would soon be awarded additional routes to Germany, but I began to long for my position in command, and the not-inconsequential increase in salary it would bring. In the autumn of 1978, I returned to my old position of Boeing 727 captain but with the realization that new aircraft were on the drawing boards of the world's aircraft manufacturers and my airline had ordered a few. Perhaps sooner than I expected, I might attain my long-held ambition to command an international oceanic flight. In the meantime I was happy to be back flying the trusty 727.

THE BOEING 727

"Truly superior pilots are those that use their superior judgment to avoid situations where they might have to use their superior skills."---Author unknown.

The Boeing 727 has often been described as the "DC-3" of the jet age. In the same way the DC-3 introduced the world to air transportation, the Boeing 727 brought the jet age to everybody. Almost every airline in the world eventually purchased this aircraft to use on routes not suitable for the longer range Boeing 707 and Douglas DC-8 aircraft. Eventually it grew to be a favorite with both pilots and passengers, but in 1965, shortly after its introduction, the flying public thought of it as a death trap.

On August 16, 1965, a United Airlines 727 crashed in Lake Michigan approaching Chicago O'Hare airport, killing all 30 on board. Less than three months later an American Airlines 727 crashed while approaching Cincinnati, killing 60 passengers and crew. Three days later, on November 11, 1965, another United Airlines 727 went down approaching Salt Lake City, killing 43 of the 85 souls on board. The public became outraged. Airlines scratched the number 727 from their timetables while others tried to disguise the aircraft type with glamorous sounding names as "Flagship" and "Mainliner".

Research done by NASA found that pilots, who were mostly transitioning from the more docile DC-6 propeller aircraft, were often caught unawares by the high descent rate of the 727, especially at night in clear weather, when the visual clues can be deceptive. With special training and the reduction of landing flap settings, this type of accident no longer occurs.

My company inherited their fleet of 727 aircraft through the purchase of Northeast Airlines in 1972. The first time I entered the cockpit of one of the adopted aircraft my heart sank. It was dirty, beat up and worn out. (Never trust anyone who tells you there is no correlation between economics and safety.) Granted, the aircraft that so disappointed me happened to be one of Northeast's oldest, a "-100" model complete with steering controls slightly offset from center for a reason only God and Boeing can know. My disappointment thankfully would abate as delivery of brand new –200 models arrived on a regular basis.

Overcoming my initial reticence about the "three holer" as we affectionately called it, I grew to appreciate its amazing performance and capabilities. As soon as newer, more powerful engines were available, Boeing lengthened the fuselage and extended its range until its capabilities exceeded the early DC-8 and B-707 models.

The wing of the 727 is a marvel of engineering. Sitting on the ground with no hydraulic power, the wing seems to disassemble itself as the leading edge droops and the trailing edge flaps sag-- looking like a cartoon caricature of a toy airplane. This complex design enabled the 727 to land at airports previously unable to accommodate jet service. An incident during my last month flying the 727 clearly illustrates this capability.

We have landed in Jackson, Mississippi in January 1982. It is snowing hard but the snow is dry and braking very good. We spend the night and expect an early afternoon departure for Atlanta. Overnight, freezing rain has replaced the snow and all inbound flights are cancelled. Jackson Airport is not equipped to remove even a flake of snow and so we spend another night sealed in our Holiday Inn motel room. On the third day, the sky is overcast, with the temperature just above freezing. We report to the airport and find our inbound flight circling above while deciding if they should attempt a landing. There is no equipment to measure braking effectiveness on the airport. In fact, there are few airports anywhere during this time that have this capability. Since no aircraft have landed for two days the Captain decides to over-fly Jackson and leave us once again in the clutches of the Holiday Inn. In my desperation to abandon Jackson, Mississippi, I call the flight on our company radio and say, "Hey, would you like me to drive the airport pickup truck down the runway at 60 MPH and check the braking?" There is a long silence. I know he is weighing the lost revenue against the possibility of sliding off the end of the runway. If our roles had been reversed I probably would have told him to go to hell. Surprisingly he says, "O.K. Give it a try, but make sure you get up to at least 60 MPH before braking."

As I walk out to the airport pickup truck, accompanied by the hesitant chief of airport maintenance, I feel my feet crunching through the thin layer of ice that collapses into the slush beneath. I am confident the weight of the aircraft will push aside the thin ice layer allowing the tires to make solid contact with the runway pavement below.

"I think I should do the driving cause I don't think we got insurance to cover you."

"Oh no problem, just make sure you get to 60 MPH before you put the brakes on."

"How come 60? Don't that plane land a lot faster'n that?"

"Yes, but it's the last few miles of speed that counts. Above 60 the pilot still has some aerodynamic control. Below that speed on ice the plane is just a sled."

"Oh."

171

As we drive out to the runway, it is obvious there is plenty of traction as the driver is barreling down the taxiway as if on dry ground. Still, my confidence begins to crumble as I realize the responsibility I am taking on. Do I really know how a 160,000-pound airplane is going to handle by comparing it to this 4,000-pound pickup? Am I jeopardizing the lives of others to satisfy my desire to abandon Jackson, Mississippi and get on with my life? Well, lets wait and see when he slams the brakes on.

Turning on to the runway the chief accelerates to 60 and puts on the brakes as if there is a boxed hot pizza on the seat beside him.

"Izzat whatcha want?"

"Uh, no. Actually what I want is for you to make a panic stop."

"O.K." This time he does a nice job of braking hard and the pickup rolls to a stop in a straight line.

"That's great, can we do it one more time down at the landing end where he will touch down?"

He does as I ask and the result is as favorable as I could hope for. I call our airborne flight on the special radio installed in the pickup and report the results to the Captain who replies; "O.K. Here we come."

I stand outside to watch the 727 as it circles to the left and then lines up on the runway. I notice he is using full flaps and his stabilized approach is perfect. My heart begins to pound as I realize if anything goes wrong my "ass is grass."

The 727 crosses over the end of the runway and immediately touches down. There is a great cloud of snow blasted forward of the aircraft, as the captain uses maximum reverse thrust. This completely obscures our view. I am in shock, as I cannot tell if he is off the runway or has come to a stop. When the snow settles, I realize the aircraft is safely on the runway, taxiing slowly. My heart races with joy, and I breathe again. The Captain has executed his landing with such precision he is forced to add power to reach the first taxiway where he can clear the runway.

The Boeing 727 has performed precisely the way the engineers designed it to perform.

We make our getaway from Jackson with a full load of happy passengers grateful to be leaving the not so "sunny south." I am feeling full of confidence and perhaps a little smug that my plan to escape Jackson went off so well. My elation however, is brief.

"Hey did ya'll hear the news about Air Florida?" It is the Air Traffic Controller calling us.

I trigger the mike button and reply, "No, we've been snowed in--in Jackson for three days."

"This just happened a few minutes ago---one of their 737's departing Washington National hit the 14th street Bridge. Apparently this weather reaches all the way to D.C.".

My mouth turns to cotton and my stomach sours. I can barely utter a reply. "Uh, thanks for the info. Let us know if you hear any more details." I am thinking there must be a famous quote from someone that covers this situation. But all I can recall is— "there is a fine line between good fortune and disaster."

Later that day, I watched, with millions of others, the taped replay of the dramatic rescue of five passengers from the icy waters of the Potomac River. 74 others did not survive. Air Florida was a new airline, spawned by deregulation. Their flight crews had limited experience in the icy winter weather of the northeast. Crash investigators determined the crew failed to use engine anti ice on takeoff which caused the engine gauges to show full power when in reality, they had far less. Deregulation has exacted a price on society that will not always be measured in dollars.

TWO ENGINES, OVERWATER

"Flying an aeroplane with only a single propeller to keep you in the air. Can you imagine that?"----Captain Picard, from Star Trek, The Next Generation.

There are those of us who view aviation as almost a religion, complete with a litany of commandments: "Thou shall not take off with unused runway behind you. Thou shall not fly low and slow. Thou shall not fly in instrument weather without proper training and a sufficiently equipped aircraft. Thou shall not fly over water or at night on one engine." The penance for violating these commandments is often death. So then, why have we decided to test the gods of aviation by operating twin-engine jet aircraft on long transoceanic routes? It is one thing to lose an engine over land where one is, at worst, only minutes from a reasonable landing place. It is quite another to find yourself over the mid-Pacific or North Atlantic oceans where a suitable landing site can be three hours away. What is so different now, that we decided to violate one of aviation's most revered rules; Thou shall not fly a single engine aircraft over water at night with revenue passengers? After all, even with two engines, sooner or later, one will fail, and with three hours to the nearest suitable landing place, you have exposed yourself to a whole new set of probabilities with only one engine remaining. Although the laws of probability allow it in the first place, the truth is that the technological marvel of the jet engine has made mince meat of the laws of probability. In 34 years of flying the line I have had only one in-flight catastrophic failure of a jet engine, and two precautionary shutdowns. In a precautionary shutdown the engine can be re-started and used in an emergency. In other words, the incident of engine failure is so low it is a risk we are willing to accept, much akin to living in an earthquake zone, or the Midwest's "Tornado Alley," or "Hurricane Gulch" in Florida and the Gulf of Mexico.

All great technological leaps are spawned by economics. And so it is with the new aircraft. The political entities that control the spigots of crude oil do not wish to see the wealth of their nations burned up at ten cents a gallon. That is what jet fuel cost when the first Boeing 747s were put in service. Airlines had to find a way to reduce the massive thirst for the now-precious jet fuel. Two engines with the power of three or four is the right answer. Perhaps we should credit OPEC for the Boeing 767, 777, and European Airbus.

1982: ELECTRIC JET

"The scientific theory I like best is that the rings of Saturn are composed entirely of lost airline luggage." ---*Mark Russell*

Fellow pilots told me that a February in Binghamton, New York, offers only three days of sunshine. During the almost two weeks in training at the Link Division of the Singer Corp., we are offered not a single ray. This is not a vacation. A small group of captains and first officers, myself included, arrived by "Weedeater," the affectionate name we give to noisy turboprop commuter aircraft, for training on my company's newest aircraft: the Boeing 767. All of us had successfully bid, and were awarded by seniority the opportunity to fly this new and technologically challenging aircraft. This fuel-conserving and efficient aircraft is going to keep my company profitable. Rumors are flying that it will one day be used in our new trans-Atlantic operation. After all, it is a wide body (double aisle), and later versions will carry as many as 300 passengers.

We are not going to fly an actual airplane while here in Binghamton; instead we will spend every day, for ten days, in a simulator built by the same company responsible for the famous WWII blind flying box I so shamefully crashed at the home of Frontier Airlines in 1963. The difference in sophistication between the old Link and the new simulator is comparable to a rowboat and the QEII ocean liner.

177

The most stunning innovation, we soon discover, is the cockpit design, which allows the aircraft to be operated safely with two pilots, thereby eliminating the second officer or flight engineer. Advanced electronics using cathode ray tube or CRT displays replace the traditional analog-clock like instruments, giving rise to the name "Glass Cockpit." Automatic monitoring systems eliminate the need for a human watchdog. It is actually more advanced in instrumentation than the space shuttle. My heart beats with pride. Perhaps even more important to the economics of this aircraft and the profitability of my company, is the reliability of its massive turbofan engines. But first, it would have to prove itself in domestic service before we dared risk misfortune over water.

Before arriving in Binghamton for simulator training, I faced the daunting ordeal of a 10-day ground school to learn the complex new systems. I know not one pilot who enjoys the tedium of learning and memorizing numbers. For me, it is absolute hell. I was naturally apprehensive. I wish now to express my gratitude to the myriad Boeing engineers who, in designing this aircraft, at last, came to their senses. What they did to gain my everlasting gratitude is eliminate the miasma of numbers for engine rpm, temperatures, pressures, over speed and under speed, numbers for pneumatics, hydraulics, electrics, and pressurization—numbers that on a dark night, in a dim cockpit with old, tired eyes rattled by clear air turbulence, can hardly be read, let alone acted upon. And what replaced all these numbers? Colors. Beautiful greens and yellows and terrifying reds. Instead of trying to figure out from a 1.5 inch diameter instrument whether or not the engine is rotating at 102 percent of rpm, a normal number, or 102.1 percent, an excessive number, the instrument lights up red, telling you, "Hey there, do something." Instead of needing to stare at a hundred gauges trying to surmise if all is well, there simply will be green. And if something is about to fall apart, run out, or go bad, there will be a yellow caution light alerting you to impending inconvenience, instead of surprising you with a loud bang, or an even-louder silent engine. If sticks, baling wire, and fabric represented the old technology, the CRT, transistor, and computer have replaced it. Thank God. And thank you, Boeing.

It is in the nature of pilots to give their aircraft a pet name. The 767, with its complex computer-generated flight instruments and advanced flight management systems, soon became "The Electric Jet."

After completing simulator training in Binghamton, our group returned to Atlanta where we each made a half dozen landings to familiarize ourselves with an actual aircraft. Boeing designed the 767 to operate at higher altitudes, therefore the wing design, long and thin, seemed more like that of a sailplane. An added benefit to this wing is very docile landing characteristics, making smooth landings more the rule than the exception.

After our landing practice I decided to check out the cabin layout. My instructor called out "hey, try flushing the toilet and see what you think." I did as told and damn near had a stroke as the loud pop of the new vacuum flush toilet startled me.

"Now wait till you see this."

Our hilarious flight instructor proceeded to unroll about twenty feet of toilet paper, leading it from the toilet bowl outside into the passenger cabin aisle.

"Now when I say go, you flush the toilet: Go!"

I flushed the toilet and watched in amazement as the vacuum from the toilet sucked the paper right into the bowl in about a nanosecond.

"A flight attendant showed me this. When they get bored they take two rolls of toilet paper and using both heads across from each other, roll the paper all the way to the rear of the airplane down each aisle and someone shouts go. Voila, a toilet paper race."

I cannot help but marvel at the ingenuity of idle minds.

DUAL QUALIFICATION

"Both optimists and pessimists contribute to the society. The optimist invents the airplane, the pessimist, the parachute. --- George Bernard Shaw

Spitfire, Mustang, Thunderbolt, Lightning. If you are an aviation aficionado those sobriquets bring to the artful eye specific images of sleek, fast, wartime fighter aircraft whose appearance befits association with such aesthetic namesakes. Alas, most attempts to give descriptive names to the mass of aluminum configured as a commercial airliner have been dismal failures. Certainly there have been some mild successes: the Lockheed Constellation and TriStar aircraft most notably, but in the main, a DC-6, DC-7, and DC-8, will always be known as just that. The same can be said of Boeing's successful line of transports starting with the 727, 737, 747, nothing more than mere numbers placed at the bottom of a draftsman's blueprint, meant only to identify it from its larger or smaller sibling. Perhaps it's just a manifestation of our technological society to dehumanize what to me should be treated as human kind's greatest expression of God's art.

During the adolescent years of the airline industry, a few halfhearted attempts were made to attach aesthetic names to the working fleet. United Airlines had its Mainliners, American Airlines its Flagships, and Eastern its Great Silver Fleet. Pan American, although no longer equipped with flying boats, called all their aircraft "Clippers." Possibly, during that time, associating your airline with a railroad or maritime enterprise might instill confidence in the nervous traveling public.

Perhaps it is the utilitarian nature of the commercial airliner that prevents the artful blending of flesh and aluminum in its description. The one exception to this paradox is the Airbus, an apt descriptive given to an entire European aircraft industry. Yet, to the eye and mind of an airline pilot, there is aesthetic beauty and emotional attachment to our aircraft. Often, we invent clever names that forsake the technical coldness, embracing the endearing attributes of our aircraft. Thus, the Boeing 737 becomes "Fat Albert," the DC-8 becomes the "Diesel Eight," and the MD-90 becomes the "Mad Dog."

My favorite aircraft is the Boeing 757. The long, graceful fuselage, balancing two massive engines from its wings, gives it a hungry, lean, mean and powerful appearance. And powerful it really is. I personally refer to it as "The Rocket." Because it must be able to fly fully loaded on one engine, its performance on two is spectacular. It began life as a replacement for the Boeing 727, and, in fact, the fuselage is a stretched modification of the venerable older 727. Boeing Aircraft decided to make the cockpit identical to the more advanced wide body 767, thereby offering the airlines two different aircraft but only one cockpit design. This could result in millions of saved training dollars. Boeing's redesign of the 757 caused a delay in delivery to my airline and the 767 arrived first.

Ordinarily, when a new aircraft is introduced, the airlines establish a training program consisting of at least two weeks of ground school, in which pilots learn the particulars of the aircraft mechanical systems. This is followed by two weeks of daily training in a simulator with sophisticated visual systems capable of simulating real-world conditions. An inspector from the Federal Aviation Administration then gives a check flight before a pilot is allowed to fly the actual aircraft. After successfully passing the check flight, the new pilot may taxi, take off and land a real airplane for a few hours. Only then can the pilot carry passengers on a regular line flight. But even that first flight must be under the supervision of a line-pilot instructor who occupies the first officer's seat. After twenty-five hours of supervised flight, he is then signed-off to command on his own without supervision. This system is the law, and applied to virtually all airline aircraft and its pilots—until the 757 came along.

Training an airline pilot is a long and expensive ordeal, the cost born by the airline and naturally passed on to the customer. The desire of Boeing Aircraft to make their product more competitive by designing identical cockpits in the 757 and 767 is a terrific idea. The problem, of course, is that the two aircraft are quite different in size and handling characteristics. The 767 is almost twice the size of the 757, and carries almost twice the passengers. Could you drive an 18-wheeler Mack truck if the steering wheel and pedals looked like your Chevrolet sedan? To answer this question, Boeing ran a test. Airline pilots trained on the 767 were put in the cockpit of a 757 (without passengers of course), and were told to fly it as if it were a 767. Since there has never been a pilot born who didn't think he could fly anything with wings (including a Mack Truck), the test was a resounding success. And so word went out: pilots were to be issued a type-rating for the Boeing 757 if they were already rated on the Boeing 767, even if they had never seen a Boeing 757!

Since I am already rated in the Boeing 767, my chief pilot ordered me to get over to the FAA office ASAP, and pick up my new rating. When I arrived, a disbelieving government secretary confronted me, stating: "You're crazy! We don't just give out type ratings here!"

My confidence sunk further when the local air carrier inspector emerged from his office having overheard our conversation, and said, "Surely you don't think we are just going to hand you a new aircraft rating without a flight test do you?"

I replied, "Sir, I am only doing what I have been told to do. Why don't you call my chief pilot and talk to him?"

"Nah," he replied. "He will just confirm what you just told us. Here, I just got this fax from Washington." He handed me a piece of paper that authorized him to issue me a type rating on the Boeing 757, even though I had never set eyes on one. His parting shot: "This is the god damnedest thing I ever heard of!"

Aware our new Boeing 757 would arrive any day, I still had not given much thought to the consequences of it being thrust upon me with no warning. As I walked toward the departure gate to board the expected 767 I instead came upon a brand new shiny 757. Staring out the terminal window, with my nose pressed to the glass in stunned silence, my first reaction is, I must be at the wrong gate. Repeated shouts of "Captain, Captain" brought me back to reality as the gate agent explained that the new airplane was a substitute for the mechanically ailing 767 that should have been parked in its place. Is everything alright?" he asked. "We were told you were qualified to fly this airplane. Is this correct?"

Feigning confidence, I recovered from temporary shock, and said, "Oh yes, of course, no problem. It's just that I have never seen …" I let my words trail off to a mumble and quickly boarded before he asked any more questions. My first officer, in no less a state of shock than I, took his seat across from mine. We said little, and looked around trying to pretend it is just like the old and familiar 767. Incredulously, we found that sure enough, it did look the same — as long as we didn't turn our heads past 90 degrees left or right. My first words to him were, "You know, I think we can do this if we don't look back!" He did not seem reassured.

A few minutes later the passengers began boarding. Inevitably, we knew, someone would stick his or her head in the cockpit to see what the new airplane looked like up front. It took only a moment before the first curious passenger entered

exclaiming "WOW! THIS AIRPLANE LOOKS BRAND-NEW
… HOW LONG HAVE YOU BEEN FLYING IT?"

Without directly answering our curious passenger's query, I
mumbled something to the effect that this airplane is just like the
767, and yes, it is brand-new and excuse us, but we have to run the
checklist. In the back of my mind I was trying to convince myself
we were not doing something immoral, illegal or unethical.

As the tug pushed us away from the boarding gate, with every
one of the 189 seats filled, I tried to pretend I am in the all-familiar
767. Forced to turn around to answer a questioning flight
attendant, my illusion is shattered. From the pilot seats rearward, I
am in uncharted waters. Forced to answer, "I don't know," to her
questions about the galley amenities, her disgusted look turned to
dismay when I confessed we had never been on a 757 before this
day. I knew we would see little of her angelic face that evening.

It is now dark outside, and I could not help feeling like a 15th
century sailor who has been told: "Don't worry, the world is not
flat, take my word for it, and keep heading west. You won't fall
off." And, of course, we did not fall off. Our takeoff, climb,
cruise and descent into Cincinnati were as normal and uneventful
as a trip to the supermarket. Only the landing turned out to be
exceptional. It was as smooth as I would ever make in the 757,
and I fell in love.

I would see much of this aircraft in the following months, and
my affection and respect would grow as she slowly revealed the
intimate secrets of her capabilities and performance. (An airplane
will forever be of the feminine gender.) She is not, however,
without fault. As in any woman of great beauty, it is desired that
her weight be kept to a minimum; therefore, carbon fiber replaced
the heavy steel brakes on her legs. This resulted in jack rabbit
stops and screechy, noisy taxiing, necessitating announced
apologies to the innocents on board who found her attractiveness
wanting. In time, this would be corrected, and her graciousness in

185

flight would be equaled when she was forced to stand on her newer, trimmer legs.

Early in my relationship with the 757, an opportunity presented itself where she could show off the power and performance instilled in her by the capable engineers of Boeing Aircraft. The venue for our exhibition is Washington, D.C., in early autumn and Congress in session.

Washington National Airport is a small, tightly packed and entirely inadequate airport whose existence is maintained only because it lies within a stone's throw of the Capitol building. Nowhere else would such compromising geography pass as satisfactory before the eyes of the harsh and critical FAA regulators. To the credit of pilots that operate in and out of National Airport, its safety record is second to none. Nevertheless, great skill and attention to detail is necessary to navigate the prescribed flight patterns, which are designed to avoid the White House and other national monuments, and keep the noise level within tolerable limits. Therefore, only the most nimble airliners, of limited capacity, are allowed to fly into Washington National Airport, recently renamed Reagan National Airport.

In 1983, the Boeing 757 emerged as the right aircraft to meet the need for greater capacity, with the capability of safe arrivals and departures at National Airport. Nimble, quiet, and with terrific performance, the 757 can carry forty more passengers than the older 727. And so I found myself, that autumn Sunday in 1983, landing at National with 189 congressman, lobbyists, and ordinary tourists. After discharging our complement of VIPs, we found that we would have only five passengers who wished to depart Washington for the return flight to Atlanta on that Sunday afternoon. This is not unusual, as the normal Washington flow is out on Friday, and in on Sunday.

When the wind blows from the north, the normal takeoff direction at National is to the north and into the wind.

186

Unfortunately, maintaining a northerly heading will take you right over the Washington Monument, the White House, and in close proximity to almost every important national treasure and government building so vital to the maintenance and glory of the free world's most populous democracy. This democracy does not want aluminum aircraft falling on its national treasures; therefore, it has established strict rules to avoid just such a catastrophe, with stiff penalties for those who do not comply.

The procedure for departing National Airport states that after takeoff and reaching the end of the runway, one is to follow the Potomac River to the northwest. After soaring 2,500 feet above the ground, power must be reduced to a level that insures the peace and tranquility of our lawmakers below who are busy with the burdens of the free world. This level of power allows only the most meager climb performance, but it must be maintained until the aircraft has either miraculously clawed its way to an altitude of 5,000 feet or has quietly crawled away from the sensitive ears of those conducting the business of government. Only then can power be re-applied to the tiptoeing engines, and normal flight resumed.

As our aircraft taxies away from the terminal building, several aircraft call on the radio with their compliments on our attractive new aircraft, for ours is one of the first of the type to appear at National Airport. Although awash in pride, I am not distracted enough to not notice how hard the wind is blowing out of the north. Turning to the first officer I say, "Robert, with this light passenger load and strong wind, I think we might be able to cross the end of the runway at 5000 feet. We wouldn't have to reduce power for noise abatement. What do you think?"

Robert is not the talkative type. He looks at me, shrugs his shoulders, and says, "Perhaps." It is all the urging I need.

Robert calls for takeoff clearance, and it is granted. We roll on to the runway, turning to face a 30-knot wind, and I apply the maximum power allowed on this cool, autumn afternoon. Our boisterous Boeing leaps into the air after only seconds on the ground. Pulling the nose up to 18 degrees pitch, our lively lady is still accelerating. Very slowly, so as not to startle the passengers, I increase the angle of climb until there is no doubt we will be at 5,000 feet before leaving the airport boundary. Over the radio there is a chorus of "ooohs" and aaahs" as I ease the nose over, and turn northwest so as not to frighten the White House staff. We knew it had to look spectacular from the ground, like nothing they had ever seen before, because no other aircraft flying out of National Airport is capable of this kind of performance. We had done nothing illegal, and we had followed the prescribed procedures. The only comment from National tower is, "GOOD SHOW! Contact departure control and have a nice day."

The Boeing 767 "Electric Jet" was popular with our passengers. Its double aisle wide body design with few center seats provided a level of comfort available up to that time only on the longer transcontinental and international routes. After its reliability was proven in domestic service, there was talk of using the 767 on our rapidly multiplying international routes. This fuel-saving new generation of aircraft helped return our airline and others to profitability after barely surviving the oil embargo and the trials and tribulations of deregulation. My vision of commanding an international aircraft across an ocean seemed to be moving toward reality. Then, in the summer of 1984, the yin and yang of fortune came into balance. One of our finest aircraft, a Lockheed TriStar, crashed at the Dallas-Fort Worth Airport, a victim of wind shear, a phenomenon only recently recognized.

As the TriStar approached DFW, with surface temperatures more than 102° F, a violent thunderstorm grew in intensity directly in front of its approach path. Unaware of the intensity of this seemingly unimportant thunderstorm, the TriStar passed directly underneath and a microburst, or blast of descending air drove the plane toward the ground. As it emerged from the edge of this thunderstorm, its airspeed dropped below a safe level, a result of

188

the descending air from the microburst creating an instant tail wind as it hit the ground and was deflected parallel to the aircraft's flight path. The Lockheed's landing gear struck the ground first on an airport perimeter road. The aircraft then careened onto the airport property, crashing head on into gigantic fuel storage tanks located a few hundred yards to the left of the landing runway. There were few survivors.

One can speculate, if only the tanks had been underground, or located even further away from the landing area, how many would have survived? I think many. However, in a shameless display of economics over safety, the tanks were rebuilt, and to this day remain in the very same spot. I do not wish to place the blame on those who construct fuel tanks, as there is plenty of blame to pass around. The air traffic controllers who directed them toward the storm, the meteorologists who failed to recognize the rapidly developing threat to arriving aircraft, and, of course, the pilots themselves who fatally assumed the thunderstorm was of little significance.

That evening, while on a layover in Los Angeles, the ultimate destination of the ill-fated flight, a phone call awakened me shortly after going to sleep in preparation for an early morning departure. Flight operations wanted to know if I could pilot a special flight of surviving relatives back to Dallas. I could not refuse, and at midnight, I boarded an aircraft filled with stunned, tearful, and brokenhearted passengers. My embarrassment was so great I could not speak to them. What could I say? What hollow words could I speak that would possibly ease their suffering? And so I said nothing, flying to Dallas with the burden of shame a part of my crew.

As we approached DFW Airport, we were cleared to land on the very runway that was the scene of the previous day's tragedy. I knew the passengers would see the path of destruction, as it would lie just off to the left of our touchdown point. I considered requesting another runway. But was this for my benefit, or theirs?

After all, they had come to face their personal tragedy directly. What right had I to ease my own burden of guilt by avoiding the sight of death and destruction? After landing, I remained in the cockpit until all had left the aircraft.

To my company's credit, they had planned for just such a disaster. It would be irresponsible of them had they not. For just as surely as there are earthquakes in California, hurricanes in Florida, or thunderstorms in Texas, there will be aircraft that bring death and destruction to innocent passengers. From all over the system, specially trained agents were assigned to each surviving family member, attending to their immediate and future needs. This gave rise to accusations that the airline was acting only in heartless self-interest, hoping to keep the lawsuits to a minimum. But I can tell you now that I knew our management well, and while it is true that it was in their interest to act as they did, they did it because it was also the right thing to do.

DECISIONS, DECISIONS, DECISIONS!

"The odds against there being a bomb on a plane are a million to one, and against two bombs a million times a million to one. Next time you fly, cut the odds and take a bomb."----Benny Hill

The early 1960s brought the first aerial hijackings. Crazed Cubans had suddenly wanted to go home. Soon all manner of maniacs decided free transportation to the homeland of their choice could be had at the point of a gun. Airlines in the United States issued their pilots special charts that showed in a few moments whether you could get to Cuba from wherever you were before running out of fuel. Most of these early events were treated as inconvenient larks, as no one had been hurt or killed. It wasn't long, however, before aerial terrorism turned deadly, and the world came face to face with a new and serious threat to the traveling public.

As security checkpoints were being erected at airports all over the world, airline crews underwent special training on how to deal with potential and actual hijackers: how to spot disguised explosive devices, and how to deal with these explosives when they were discovered. These programs were costly, but often helpful. In the final analysis, however, the decision-making capabilities of the crew often determined the outcome.

In one notorious early incident, a hijacker was overcome and shot dead by an armed passenger while the aircraft remained parked on the ground. The captain of the 747 flight threw the hijacker's body out of the 30-foot high passenger door, and was later sued by the hijacker's next of kin for unusual cruelty. I thought the captain's anger a natural reaction under the circumstances.

My own company became the victim of multiple hijackings that in one tragic case resulted in the death of a fellow crewmember, the death of a security guard, and the serious wounding of the captain of the flight.

In 1973, at the Baltimore Washington Airport, a maniacal gunman shot his way past the security guard, killing him, and then boarded the DC-9 awaiting departure. Pointing the gun at the pilots, he ordered them to "get this airplane out of here." They did as they were told, but after starting the engines, they found no driver for the tug that pushes the aircraft away from the gate. Several passengers had escaped the aircraft before the hijacker ordered the door closed. Increasingly nervous over the delay, the hijacker shot and killed the first officer, turned to the pilot, and said, "Do something or I will kill you, too." The captain put the engines in reverse in an attempt to back away from the gate. However, the DC-9, still attached to the tug, went nowhere. The gunman then shot the captain, seriously wounding him. Airport police arrived on the scene, and when the hijacker appeared behind the passenger door to look outside, the police shot him through the door, killing him.

Five years passed before the captain recovered enough to return to the flight deck. He later told an acquaintance he could see the bullet leave the gun when the gunman fired. A sad footnote to this affair occurred years later when the captain of that fateful Baltimore flight was forced into early retirement when his behavior became erratic. His record prior to the shooting had been impeccable. Under the heading, "There but for the grace of God, go I," is the fact that I flew the exact same flight the following evening, and would have been on the doomed flight but for fate, and perhaps, seniority.

192

As the '70s passed into the '80s, increased security measures reduced hijacking incidents to a manageable level. A new problem however arose, giving the airline industry fits. Prank bomb threats became as frequent as lost luggage.

Remember when you were a kid and would call the grocery store, and ask if they had Prince Albert in a can? Well, the modern version of that is to call an airline and say: "There's a bomb on flight XXX." Everyday, airlines the world over receive calls similar to this. The ability to sort out the seriousness of each call is important to the well-being of any airline. To treat each as a serious threat would bring the industry to a standstill. To ignore all of them is to take on unacceptable risk. So, in each case, someone has to make a decision to treat the call as a prank or as a true terrorist threat, and often that someone is the captain. In 1986, I faced exactly this situation.

That evening I commanded a Boeing 767 departing Ft. Lauderdale, Fla. for New York City. Five minutes before departure, with all passengers, baggage, and cargo on board, I was quietly called from the cockpit by the senior agent, and told to go to operations to take an important phone call from a company official. While I didn't think my company fired their pilots five minutes before departure, I could sense this telephone call did not contain good news. I picked up the phone handset and said, "This is Ippolito. What's up?"

"Captain, this is flight control. We have a telephoned bomb threat for a Flight XXX. (I am using XXX rather than the actual flight number.) "You are the only Flight XXX operating, so here are the facts. The call came into our San Francisco reservation center. No airline was given, no city, departure, destination or time mentioned. Just, there is a bomb on flight XXX, and then a hang-up. Since your flight is about to depart, we thought you should know. Whaddya wanna do?"

193

What do I want to do? Well, hell, let's just get all the passengers off the plane, and all their baggage, and all the cargo, and search each piece, and each passenger, then we will search the aircraft, and if all goes well we should be ready to go the day after tomorrow! I am sure the passengers will understand when we tell them some idiot in San Francisco has decided to shut down the airline system with a local phone call.

On the other hand, we could just treat this as another prank call and ignore it. However, the lives of 250 people are possibly riding on my decision. Do I want to be responsible for the deaths of 250 passengers and eight crewmembers because I think this is a crank call? But then, can we let ourselves be held hostage by a juvenile delinquent? My company could well go out of business if we stopped to check every flight every time someone got the urge to be mischievous.

All these thoughts were racing through my mind as flight control waited for my decision. I asked him how many bomb threats did he know about that night, and he answered, "Including the other airlines, fifteen, but your flight number is the only one that matched a caller's." I then sought his input by asking, "What would you do?" He would have none of it, and replied, "Captain, that's why they pay YOU the big bucks and not me!"

So what did I do? I weighed the probabilities that a call made a continent away, and one of at least fifteen made that night, might be just a prank, against the horrible reality of it turning out to be real. I considered the consequences to my company, and the entire airline industry being held hostage by pranksters, and I considered the tragic consequences of a real bomb being on our aircraft. I made my decision, but I cannot tell you that decision, because to do so would only lend credibility to both the prankster and the terrorist. What would you do? Think it over. I can say only that my passengers arrived at their destination safely.

56 NORTH 10 WEST, TIME REMAINING 1:54

"If God wanted us to fly, He would have given us tickets." ----
Mel Brooks

Gordon contacts Scottish Oceanic Control on our VHF radio. We are 149 nautical miles from Machrihanish, well within radar coverage and reliable radio communication. We are becoming more an aircraft, and less a boat. Still, we use the language of mariners even though soon below us there will be only solid earth. The use of nautical miles in aviation has a practical use. One nautical mile equals one minute of latitude, and therefore offers a useful unit of measurement. I know not what practical basis exists for the ordinary statute mile, except that it is 5,280 feet in length.

Scottish control informs us we are in radar contact. This means we can put away our plotting chart. We no longer need to make position reports, as the separation of our aircraft from others will now be in the hands of the Scottish controller. There is a noticeable relaxation of tension in the cockpit, as we are now "feet dry," and any emergency will not likely end with a landing on water.

The sky to the northeast rapidly grows brighter as the sun races toward our side of the earth. If we land toward the east in Frankfurt, which is our desire, it will save ten minutes of flying time. However, the sun will fill the windshield, decreasing our forward visibility as the rays are scattered and reflected by the particles of smoke, haze and fog that are forecast upon our arrival.

195

Behind the cockpit, passengers soon will be awakened by cabin lights brought up from their overnight dimmed position. There will be the clanking of dishes, and the rumble of food carts as flight attendants prepare breakfast for those whose hunger was satiated only a few hours ago with dinner on the other side of the world.

As the sky brightens, so does the conversation in the cockpit. It is as though we, too, had just awakened from a night's sleep, and it is a new day. Keyes mentions that nothing has been heard from our boisterous "rock star." Gordon concurs and mumbles something about not having to write an explanatory letter for the company files. For myself, I am the most grateful of all, for it is the captain's responsibility, when all is not "tranquil and serene" in the passenger cabin, to write an explanatory letter detailing the situation, and to forward it to the chief pilot's office. No pilot relishes this duty, for in attempting to explain a problematic situation, it suggests that we've somehow failed in our duties in command, and the company wants to know why. Adding insult to injury, this letter now becomes a permanent part of our personal file, examined whenever management wishes to judge our fitness for command.

Fortunately, I've only had to submit such a letter twice in my career. One incident that caused my company to demand an explanation happened during my favorite time of year, A time when most passengers are of good cheer. I optimistically mark it as the exception that proves the rule.

* * *

It is Christmas Eve, 1982; a day usually of merriment and good feelings toward one another. Our aircraft, a Boeing 767 is parked securely at a gate in Atlanta, Georgia. Scheduled departure time has long passed and we still have not boarded all our passengers. There seems to be an unusual amount of activity just

196

behind the cockpit near the forward passenger door. I glance back and notice the senior flight attendant, the passenger service agent, in his bright red coat, and a male passenger conversing and gesturing in a manner that suggest anything but "good cheer." Their conversation is difficult to decipher but I can tell they are not wishing each other a Merry Christmas. The flight attendant is very experienced and I am confident she will handle the problem in a professional and courteous manner. Indulging in wishful thinking gives way to reality when she bursts into the cockpit and blurts out; "Captain, this asshole just showed up and is demanding a "no smoking" seat and there are no more left." She pauses to reach down to rub her toes and continues her tirade. "Besides, the bastard stepped on my foot and it hurts like hell." In an attempt to show sympathy, I ask her a few questions. "Why is he so late?"

"His connecting flight was late."

"One of our flights?"

"No, I think Air Florida... I'm not sure. Damn, my foot hurts."

"Is the agent taking care of the problem?"

"I think so."

I glance back toward the passenger cabin and notice that the agent and the gentleman in question have proceeded to the back of the plane. "It looks like things are getting resolved back there. Are you all right?"

"Yes, I'll be o.k." And she leaves the cockpit to tend to the passengers who, I sense, are losing their Christmas spirit.

My sigh of relief is cut short when the red-coated agent storms into the cockpit and announces: "Captain, I have tried in every way to be reasonable with this man but it isn't working. He is seated in

197

the last smoking row and insists we move the smoking section one row forward. The other passengers in that row are outraged and pissed off because they bought smoking seats. He says he is a lawyer and knows his rights and will not be seated until the smoking sign is removed from his row."

With my patience running out I tell the agent, "Throw him off, we're 30 minutes late already."

"Roger Cap, I'll call the airport police right now."

I glance to my right toward the first officer who sits in serenity in his sheepskin-covered seat. In my best tenor voice I begin to sing "Joy To The World—The Lord Has"—but I am interrupted by the authoritative bustle of the Airport Police boarding our aircraft. They march resolutely toward economy class and I await the dramatic termination of the conflict. It is not to be. In short order the police, with the same authoritative demeanor as when they entered, are now marching forward toward the cockpit.

"Captain, we gotta real problem back there. This guy's got his family with him and he won't budge. He says we'll have to bodily carry all of them off the airplane unless he gets a no smoking seat."

"Well, are you going to?"

"We will if you promise to prosecute. We are not bouncers for Delta Air Lines. Besides, it's going to be messy."

This information hits me right in the gut. I do not have the authority to guarantee prosecution. I don't even know who does. Where in the hell are the Federal Aviation Regulations when I need them. So once again, the buck has stopped---right in my lap.

As the police wait patiently, I ponder my alternatives, which seem few. I am dealing with a bunch of Yankees, anxious to get home for Christmas and being half Yankee myself (I was born in Philadelphia) I am also getting angry.

"O.K., I'll go back there and see what I can do."

I recall the incident a few years ago with the children who started a food fight. Perhaps this technique might work with adults who are acting like children. So with my hat on straight and my multi striped uniform coat buttoned, I march into economy class and face a riot. They have chosen sides, smokers facing forward, nonsmoker's rearward. There are no punches being thrown but the verbiage is intense, vehement and above all loud. I stand there with my balled hands on my hips and wait for silence. It grows quiet, just like when you were a kid and your father walked into the room and caught you doing something forbidden. They all turn to stare at me. They sense resolution at hand but are unsure how it will come about. Perhaps they were anticipating a soft conciliatory voice, one that might reassure them that, after all, they really hadn't been that bad, had they? Not tonight. Not on this Christmas Eve. And not from this pissed off Captain.

"ARE YOU ALL NUTS?" I shout this in the most punitive patriarchal voice I can find. "DO YOU WANT TO GO TO NEW YORK OR NOT?" A chorus of "Yes, oh please, yes," rises above the battlefield.

"YOU"…With my arm as straight and rigid as possible, I point directly toward the obstinate passenger, "TAKE THAT SEAT NOW SO WE CAN GO TO NEW YORK." It is as though my finger were a baseball bat, knocking him to his seat.

I turn away from the battle scene and literally push one flight attendant, two policemen and a red-coated agent ahead of me and out of the economy cabin. "Get off this airplane and close the door. We're going to New York. They did, we departed and that was that. Well, not quite.

Perhaps two months later I received the dreaded query letter from our legal department. "Dear Captain.....could you explain......in your own words.....Christmas Eve.....the incident...etc...etc. Our late arriving lawyer had written to our company president explaining the horror endured on the infamous evening. In his letter he told of the many injustices he had been subjected to from the flight attendant, the police, and the red-coated agent. Strangely enough, he credited me with "resolving the disagreement" whereas everyone else had treated him shabbily. Now I must write the dreaded explanation that probably no one will ever read, but will find its way into my personal file. I decide to make it brief as I am composing it seated in the cockpit while the passengers are boarding. The Chief Pilot's secretary will type it up later for presentation.

About half way through my literary masterpiece I begin to laugh as I recall the utter ridiculousness of the situation and I decide to embellish the tome with artistic license. Hell, no one is going to read it anyway. A few years later it would appear on bulletin boards system-wide as the perfect solution to on-board passenger problems, thankfully with the author's name blacked out. I present it here in all its rawness and poor sentence structure.

INTRA-COMPANY MEMO

To: Chief pilot
From: Capt. W. L. Ippolito

Subject: Riot on Flight 818, Dec. 24, 1982

Dear Sir;

Mr. Doe's letter seems correct as far as far as the order of events as relayed to me by the flight attendant and agent. I could not hear his conversation but the flight attendant said to me Mr. Doe was obnoxious and had stepped on her foot during one of the

200

discussions. Just as I thought the situation had been resolved by finding Mr. Doe a no smoking seat, the agent approached me in frustration and said now he wants seats together. By now we are at least 15 minutes late. The agent said, " I would like to have him removed as there is no satisfying him and he won't sit down. I agreed, as it seemed the responsible thing to do if we were ever going to depart.

The agent then said he would not get off. The passengers were mad, he was shouting and should we call the police. Well, I thought if he won't get off, won't sit down, won't take a no smoking seat, then call the police. So I supported the agent.

The police came and he still would not get off. The police would not remove him unless they got Delta's guarantee they would prosecute. The police and agent were looking at me for a guarantee.

I could see the agents were losing their confidence, the police were reluctant, the passengers angry, Mr. Doe was confused and nervous, the crisis at a deadlock. So I did what any Delta Captain would do. I put on my hat. With my hat on straight, my tie cinched up, I proceeded to order the first officer to the rear. Unfortunately, he had locked himself in the John. Seeing no way out, I marched boldly to the back right into a near riot.

Knowing I was dealing with Yankees and being half one myself, I began to shout even louder than they. *Does anyone here want to go to New York?* Yes they shouted back. *Do you want to go to New York?* I pointed to Mr. Doe. Yes he said. *Then have a seat and we'll go to New York,* I said.

He sat. I left. The police left. The agents left. The plane left.

Sincerely

Captain W. L. Ippolito

MACRIHANISH, TIME REMAINING 1:35

"The only time you can have too much fuel is when you are on fire." Author unknown.

"Damn!" Keyes curses. He has run out of lead in his pencil. I am not surprised.

"Are you writing a novel or what?" I gently chide.

"Yes, mine Kapitan, and it is now complete. According to the last chapter you are now safe for a climb to 37,000 feet."

This is Keyes' way of telling me we have burned off enough weight in fuel that our aircraft can safely operate at a higher, more efficient altitude. Since takeoff from LAX we have consumed 158,200 lbs. of precious fuel. This equates to about 23,612 gallons, purchased at a cost of approximately 50 cents per gallon. We still have 50,800 pounds of fuel remaining in our eight fuel tanks, a sufficient amount to continue to our destination, and attempt a landing. Should we be forced to abort our landing attempt because of deteriorating weather or airport equipment failure, we'll still have enough fuel to proceed to our alternate airport at Düsseldorf, and to our second alternate airport at Cologne. We will not run out of fuel.

The lyrical brogue of the Scottish controller gives way to the cockney dialect of the London controller. I am mildly surprised as the London controllers usually speak the most impeccable English

203

I have ever heard. I remember vividly my first radio transmission to London Control Center in 1978 and the controller's articulate and aristocratic reply. "Good morning Delta Lima Ten. You are re-cleared to London Gatwick Airport via ..." I don't remember the exact routing, only his polished voice, and majestic intonation. If there had been a King of England at the time I would have sworn I was speaking to him.

Oddly enough, before 1978, standard radio practice in domestic U.S. service did not include a salutary greeting. You did not hear, "Good morning, Cincinnati," or "Good evening, Chicago." I grew accustomed to the civility of the London controllers and I quickly adopted the practice myself when I returned to domestic flying. Happily, I can report that the practice seems to have caught on in the United States, adding a touch of civility and respect to pilot-controller radio communications.

As our aircraft levels off at FL 370 I marvel at the machine that has carried us safely over inhospitable terrain and endless ocean. This particular aircraft, ship number 763, (it is never referred to as aircraft number 763) is one of the last constructed by Lockheed Aircraft Corp. The original owner, Air Canada, had no need for an aircraft with such extended range and my company purchased it for use on very long distance flights. That it is in immaculate condition revealed a caring, but brief history, with its former owner. The same cannot be said of earlier aircraft my company acquired from Pan Am, an airline beset with misfortune and financial distress.

"Delta 58, the aircraft ahead of you about 20 miles just reported light to moderate turbulence at your altitude." It is the London controller offering valuable information. I reach overhead and push a small, expensive square switch that illuminates the Fasten Seat Belt sign.

Turbulence makes passengers nervous. That is why we use the euphemism "bumpy." It seems friendlier and less violent. The truth is, turbulent air is seldom a danger to flight. It is dangerous however to the passenger who chooses to ignore the seat belt sign while strolling nonchalantly about the cabin. I recall one incident in my career where in flight turbulence turned a routine flight into one of misery.

1980, NEW YORK

My eyes scan the computer generated flight plan handed to me by the LaGuardia Airport operations agent, and they fall on the line "possible light to occasionally moderate turbulence forecast." While I am not alarmed at this information, the realization that our passengers may not get the smooth and comfortable flight they expect puts me on alert. Our flight to New Orleans is lengthy and there is a meal service planned. I discuss the situation with the flight attendant in charge and let her know I will relay as much information as possible. It is one thing to suffer a bumpy flight and quite another to have it happen during a full meal service.

Our departure is uneventful and the 727 easily climbs to Flight Level 310. It is not smooth. From the moment after takeoff the air is choppy and uncomfortable. Not enough to make a seasoned flyer sick, but just enough to suggest it could get worse. I am hesitant to turn the seat belt sign off, though I realize the inevitable call of nature is importuning on at least one third of our passengers. Instead, I make an announcement explaining that we expect the bumpy air to continue for some time and ask that everyone please remain in their seats. I do this with the full knowledge that when the time comes, no passenger who has reached the limit of tolerance is going to be deterred in his or her quest for relief.

The turbulence gets worse, and we query other flights in our vicinity. I consult with our meteorology department by radio and am given little consolation. There is no smooth air. In desperation, we climb to a higher altitude. It is no better and in fact slightly worse. The minutes slip into hours and still we cannot find smooth air. Perhaps it is a blessing that no one has been served a single drop of liquid.

A flight attendant calls to ask, "When is this going to end?"

For the first time in my flying career I must honestly answer, "I don't know, maybe not until we land," as every report I receive offers no relief from the relentless motion that now is making a few passengers ill.

I check our fuel supply and consider the possibility of very low altitude flight to escape the unending choppiness. Our aircraft will consume fuel at almost twice the rate at the low altitudes where I suspect we might find smooth air. Now I must check the weather in New Orleans, as our low altitude flight will eat into our reserve fuel making a landing in New Orleans our only alternative. Once again there is a call from a flight attendant. "We really have some sick puppies back here, do you think it's going to let up?" I tell her of my newly hatched plan to seek relief at a lower altitude and I sense it has given her an ounce of hope.

We descend to 12,000 feet and still we are battered and shaken by the ceaseless turbulence. Mercifully, we will soon arrive at our destination where our passengers can once again set foot on solid ground. It will not be as easy as I expect.

Approaching the New Orleans Airport, where the weather shows cloud cover but good visibility, I am in awe that the constant turbulence has not eased even the slightest. In fact, it is getting worse. If this had been a normal flight I would have abandoned the approach and proceeded to our alternate airport. It is too late for that now. We have used our reserve fuel in the fruitless search for smooth air. Besides, we have so many sick passengers this has almost become an emergency landing.

At three miles from the airport I can see the runway. What I cannot see is my flight instruments. The shaking is now so intense that my flight instruments are a blur. I ask the first officer to call out my airspeed if he is able. His attempts are sincere, but of little use. I am flying truly by the seat of my pants, which is being battered mercilessly by the rough air. Crossing the end of the runway I am on the limit of control. From experience I know there is often a cushion of air between the wings and the ground that allows one to maintain control at the critical point of touchdown. I am counting on this natural phenomenon to assist me at touchdown. Gratefully, I am not disappointed as the air suddenly abandons its fury, allowing our beaten aircraft to settle on solid ground.

As the aircraft slows to taxi speed and the cacophony of reverse thrust abates, the silence is overwhelmed by loud applause emanating from the passenger cabin. Our relieved customers are so grateful to be alive and on the ground they have already forgotten the misery I have put them through. For me there is little joy in their applause as I am disappointed that I have subjected so many to so much.

1987

"Never stop being a kid. Never stop feeling and seeing and being excited with great things like air and engines and sounds of sunlight within you. Wear your little mask if you must to protect you from the world but if you let that kid disappear you are grown up and you are dead. ----Richard Bach, Nothing by Chance. 1963

I stand in disbelief staring at the bulletin board in the pilot lounge where I see my name listed on a teletype message indicating I have successfully bid, and been awarded (according to my seniority) a position as Captain, L-10, ATL. In plain English, this means I will be trained to fly our largest aircraft, the Lockheed L-1011 TriStar in domestic service based in Atlanta, Ga. Despite my nearly 24 years of experience, I did not believe I had the seniority to win such a position, and I am surprised that my insolent bid has been rewarded.

After the initial shock subsides, I begin to feel guilty, having just recently been promoted to line check airman for the Boeing 767, and 757 aircraft. This is an entry-level management position that requires additional training, paid for at great expense by my company. The guilt subsides somewhat as colleagues assure me that had they been in my position they would have done the same thing. After all, this is a promotion of the highest order. My company believes I am qualified to fly the largest and most complicated aircraft in their fleet. Not incidentally, this is also the best paying aircraft we operate.

Once again I must bear the misery of another ground school. The Lockheed TriStar is the most complex aircraft any airline has ever flown. Its control system allows automatic landings as smooth as can be accomplished by the most expert pilot under the most ideal conditions. It doesn't need ideal conditions to consistently perform in this manner. The complexity of its systems requires a high degree of maintenance, and is one of the reasons some airlines abandoned it for less complex aircraft with less capability. My company, however, needs this enhanced, all-weather capability as we operate into many East Coast and European cities where poor winter weather and low visibility are the norm rather than the exception. Although I had completed TriStar ground school nine years previously as a first officer, the burden of command will demand a higher level of competence than expected as second in command. This new responsibility will test the limits of my ability. Failure would be beyond humiliation.

For an agonizing two weeks, eight hours a day, instructors reveal the mystery of Lockheed's version of pneumatics, electronics, aerodynamics, hydraulics and flight control systems. There is a joke going around that Lockheed's design philosophy is "never use one switch for control when you can use two." I find the joke disgustingly un-funny. Nevertheless, I successfully complete the ground school, and pass the three-hour FAA oral exam. I have found a new love—one whose capability still, at the dawn of the new century, is unsurpassed.

Thankfully, the risk of killing yourself while learning to fly an aircraft is a relic of the past. The Lockheed TriStar simulator will never leave the ground, nor will it fall on unsuspecting ground-bound innocents. Housed in a six-story building, the simulator consists of a box-shaped flight station supported by immense hydraulic jacks that tilt and turn the cockpit in a weak imitation of flight. Once inside the simulator, however, everything seems more realistic, including the tension. To train for my new assignment, I will have to spend six hours a day for 10 days practicing the emergency procedure for every type of disaster the engineers at

Lockheed could imagine. The fact is, of course, that when an accident happens, it usually stems from a failure unforeseen by even the most prescient minds. In aviation, "Murphy's Law" claims its share of victims.

On the 10th day, an inspector from the Federal Aviation Administration, air carrier division, has the discretion to anoint me with the credentials that say I'm qualified to pilot the Lockheed L-1011, even though I have yet to see a real airplane.

At this point, as far as the government is concerned, I can take the left seat of a regularly scheduled passenger flight, fly the aircraft to its destination, and land it without any training in a real aircraft. However, I would not be in command. An experienced line check pilot seated to my right will actually command the plane, though acting as my first officer. While this practice saves a considerable amount of money in flight-training costs, my company frowns on "practicing" with passengers aboard. So instead, they take a spare aircraft off the line, and use it for flight training. Six pilots, including one flight instructor, and myself are allowed to take off, and land the empty TriStar as if it were our own personal $50 million toy, therefore risking only our own lives, and the fortune of the company.

Before I can be in command of a regular scheduled line flight I must gain 25 hours of initial operating experience under the watchful eye of a line check airman. I choose to fly with a pilot of great skill and character, Bud McIntyre. I displace him from the left seat, and he moves to the right seat to serve as my first officer while maintaining overall command of our scheduled flight from Atlanta to the island of Bermuda. We enjoy a relaxed atmosphere in the cockpit, reminiscing about the old days on the DC-6 when he was the co-pilot, and I the flight engineer. We are carrying a full airplane of 302 happy, vacation-bound souls, and 10 flight attendants to the balmy Atlantic island.

As I look down the length of the runway, I am fully confident. What I'm seeing and experiencing now is not that different from the simulator where I have spent so many hours in training. Once airborne, however, the similarities end. At 130 knots airspeed, I begin my rotation. Our TriStar lifts gently into flight, and my spirits soar. We have the engines at full takeoff thrust, but we can only maintain that setting for two minutes, lest we overstress the finely engineered steel turbine wheels, which are surrounded by the hot gases of combustion. New to this machine, but not to flight, I glance toward the instrument panel for important readings. I see a blip on the number-two engine N2 rpm indicator, then hear a crescendo of noise followed by a final bang. I feel the control wheel vibrating in my hands, while being thrust forward against my shoulder harness. This is a sensation I have never experienced, as it cannot be simulated in an electronic box. We decelerate as rapidly as if we had slammed on the brakes while on the ground. Flying the airplane is always the first action in any emergency, so I lower the nose slightly to maintain airspeed.

"Number two is failing," I call out. "Execute the engine failure check list." I have already pulled back the throttle to idle, and Bud is in the process of shutting down our very sick engine. Despite the circumstances, an air of calmness pervades our cockpit, because after all, this takeoff has been no different than most of the others I have experienced the past two weeks. In the background I can hear the Atlanta tower say, "You have flames coming from your center engine." We are too busy to respond but I am thinking, "Yes there is fire, and along with it are a bunch of very expensive engine parts descending on the Georgia countryside." Strangely there is no fire-warning bell. The destruction of our engine is so rapid and complete there is nothing left to burn.

Perhaps that contributed to the air of calm we are experiencing. We are quickly jarred back to reality by someone ringing the cockpit call bell. It is the senior flight attendant, desperate for information. "Please can you make some sort of announcement!" she demands. Well, of course, we can. After all, our passengers deserve to know that their vacation is on hold, that we will return to the airport to take care of a "maintenance problem" and that we will advise them later when we have "more information." It is difficult to practice skilled public relations while in control of a wounded aircraft, when our primary concern is to not kill our passengers or ourselves. Their vacation plans are far from our minds, as our immediate goal is to return safely to our takeoff point. Landing safely seems vacation enough.

Because of a minimal fuel load, our landing weight falls within the safety requirements for landing. We immediately circle the airport, and are given landing priority. Although our landing speed is higher than normal, due to the unburned fuel on board, we land smoothly, and without incident. I hear applause from the cabin, and can empathize with our passengers' relief. Four airport fire department vehicles follow us to the gate where mechanics stand by to perform their mechanical autopsy.

McIntyre shuts down the remaining engines, and we sit in silence as the passengers deplane. Then, because something needs saying, he says it: "Well, I didn't intend this to be a test, but in any case I think we passed!"

The lead mechanic makes his way to the cockpit with his right hand extended, and I foolishly think he wants to shake mine; but instead, I hear him say: "Captain, you might want to keep these as souvenirs." In the palm of his extended right hand he holds a small mound of tiny BB-size titanium balls. Essentially, these are all that is left of our $3 million engine. "I collected these from the tail pipe. This airplane won't be going to Bermuda today."

We depart our wounded bird for another more airworthy. The company somehow managed to find another $50 million Lockheed TriStar lying around doing nothing, so they assigned it to our Bermuda flight. On further examination, I am sure I would have discovered that another flight was cancelled in favor of ours because the revenue on our flight is greater than that of the cancelled flight. American free enterprise and a market economy can brutalize those who draw the short straw.

As I pass among the passengers on my way to our new aircraft, I don't detect panic, fear or nervousness. In fact, they look relaxed and calm, although several are complaining of the delay in their vacation plans. Perhaps it's just as well, I think to myself. After all, it is our job to get them there safely, and without alarm. It seems we have done just that. I later found out I had seriously misjudged the serenity of the 301 souls we later carried without incident to Bermuda. The passenger who would have been number 302 went home. It seems he'd had all the vacation he needed.

After leaving Bermuda, we continued on to New York, where at the end of the day we "chewed and reviewed" our Atlanta adventure. Slowly, we came to the realization that this incident marked the first time any of us had experienced catastrophic engine failure on a jet transport aircraft. Yes, we all had experienced failure of piston and turboprop engines, and perhaps an occasional precautionary shutdown before. But the pure jet turbine engine performs so reliably that most pilots never experience this kind of failure. Happily, I can report that after 34 years of flying the line, this remained for me the one and only total failure of a jet engine. Also, as far as I know, it is the only time a catastrophic failure of a jet engine occurred during a captain's first line flight. Lucky me.

In a hurry to accumulate the required 25 hours initial operating experience, I spent the next five days flying domestic routes between Atlanta, New York, and Florida. On the sixth day I returned home to be accosted by a blathering neighbor who couldn't wait to tell me about the crash she'd heard about.

"My friend was in Bermuda, and her airplane nearly crashed. Didn't you hear about it?"

"No, I did not," I replied.

"It was in the papers—here, read this."

She handed me a photocopy of a newspaper article whose headline blared: "302 passengers escape death en route to Bermuda." The newspaper is the Hamilton Bermuda Royal Gazette, a daily paper. The article went on to quote several of the deplaning passengers, who related their experience in Atlanta with varying degrees of fear, panic and terror. I seriously had misjudged my human cargo.

Not wanting to get into a discussion with my nervous neighbor, and anxious to get inside my house I said: "You know, you can't believe everything you read in the paper. They exaggerate like crazy." I returned the article she had given me and said, "For instance, I know for a fact there were only 301 on board that flight." I closed the door behind me, carefully but quickly.

During my first year flying the Lockheed TriStar, I remained landlocked in domestic service. I watched in envy as my more senior brethren operated into Germany, France, England and Ireland. At the same time, I watched in dismay as deregulation and poor management grounded once-proud airlines. Gone from the skies were Braniff and Eastern Airlines. Continental Airlines fell under brutal new management that fired their employees, declared bankruptcy, and then rehired those willing to return at half pay. TWA, in order to avoid bankruptcy, sold its London routes to American Airlines. What once existed as America's greatest airline, Pan American Airways, the airline I had dreamed of working for, had mismanaged itself to a point that no one gave it a chance to survive.

A friend once said to me, "I may be stupid, but I am smart enough to know when I am lucky." His homily rings true for me as I look at the chaos in the airline industry. What quirk of fate sent me to Atlanta instead of San Francisco or New York? What star shone when the most financially sound and best-managed airline in the world decided to offer me employment? As another friend often said: "Luck is always superior to skill."

As the Baby Boom generation approached middle age, demand for air travel soared. In a burst of expansion to meet this demand, my company acquired the financially troubled Western Airlines, a company with extensive routes to Hawaii and Mexico. Almost simultaneously, the government awarded our new entity routes to Japan, Korea and Taiwan. Usually an airline buyout or merger creates chaos, layoffs and disruption. This merger proved an exception, however, as our sum became greater than our parts. The almost daily announcement of new service to distant and exotic places is music to the ears of an airline pilot: only through growth and expansion can he hope to advance under the strict rules of seniority that exist in our industry. Since air travel was still in its youth, retirements were not yet a big factor. Now, time and circumstance were meeting to fulfill my long-held dream.

In October 1988, I successfully bid for an international captain position on our new Pacific routes to Japan, Korea and Taiwan. One of these new routes from Portland, Ore. to Seoul, South Korea, would stretch the limits of our aircraft, the Lockheed TriStar-500. Flight times often exceeded 12 hours, and during the winter months, with strong seasonal headwinds, we more than once had to stop in Japan for fuel. My company purchased the TriStar-500s from United Airlines who had purchased them from Pan American, along with all of Pan American's Pacific routes. They were some of the newest aircraft Pan American owned but they were poorly maintained.

I saw it as an ironic twist of fate that I now operated equipment once belonging to Pan American, in an area of the world in which they had once been so dominant. People worldwide had long viewed Pan American World Airways as America's flagship airline. A pioneer of transoceanic flying, Pan Am ushered in the transatlantic jet age, which inspired the Boeing

216

747. Sadly, in December 1988, Pan Am's era of dominance sustained a fatal hit, when a group of madmen chose to blow up one of its international flights over the Scottish village of Lockerbie. Not only did the terrorists murder 270 people, they also killed an entire airline.

FLIGHT ACROSS THE PACIFIC

Our altitude is 37,000 feet; the outside air temperature is minus 60 degrees, and I'm pressing my chin against the cockpit glare shield, staring at the Boeing 747 that is less than two miles ahead, and 2000-feet above. You would expect to see contrails streaming from the four engines, but not this time. She is blowing smoke rings: little, round, jewel-like circles that sparkle in the overhead sun. They are evenly spaced, but intermittent, flowing from each engine as if little men sitting on the wing drew from a mighty cigarette, puffing their cheeks then tapping it with their fingers like we all did in our teens. Off to the right is Sakhelin Island, home of the Russian Air Force. It seems only yesterday (though it has been ten years) that Korean Airlines Flight 007 was shot out of the sky near our present position. The unlucky Korean crew entered a wrong number in their navigation system, and paid the ultimate price for their carelessness. Relations thankfully are a little bit better between our countries now, and the Russians have promised not to shoot down any more civilian airliners. This revelation is only mildly comforting, and I find myself re-plotting our position on our navigation chart to steel my confidence.

The north Pacific sky has a different look when compared to the North Atlantic. It appears colder with a harder blue. Surprisingly, there is a layer of haze on the horizon—perhaps remnants of ash spewed into the atmosphere from countless active volcanoes. It has been two years since Mount St. Helens erupted near Portland, and since then volcanoes in Mexico and the Philippines have sent their abrasive refuse skyward to eat away engine parts and scar windshields and windows in airliners all over the world.

219

Soon, we will make an approach to Tokyo's Narita Airport, a relatively new facility, which is carved from precious farmland, triggering daily protests from local farmers. The three of us in the cockpit begin to discuss the inevitable confusion soon to occur when we attempt communication with Narita Approach Control. The Oriental tongue does not easily form the English words comprising the language of international aviation, nor is the Western ear receptive to the Asians' attempts at communication. We decide that all three of us will listen to every transmission and response, and if anyone does not agree with the content, we will request clarification. We all have a good laugh as the first officer passes on a story about Japan Airlines pilots who faced similar difficulties departing San Francisco several years ago.

The Japan Airlines pilot was receiving a clearance to Honolulu while awaiting departure from San Francisco. It is mandatory that the pilot receiving the clearance read it back to the controller issuing the clearance so there is no possibility of confusion. Thus the Japanese pilot, having some difficulty with the pronunciation of his destination city Honolulu, read back "Japan Airlines is cleared to Pearl Harbor, as filed, maintain 5,000 feet."

The controller, perhaps a veteran of World War II, would not let him off so easily and goaded him by saying, "That's Honolulu, Sir."

"Roger," replied the Japanese pilot, "Understand Pearl Harbor".

The San Francisco controller would not let up and repeated: "Honolulu, Honolulu".

The irritated Japanese pilot then replied, "We find it once, we will find it again."

220

Mt. Fuji beckons in the distance, much as it did for Doolittle's raiders in 1942, and I marvel at the changed geo-political world the jet airliner has wrought.

We make our approach, landing without incident and soon find ourselves seeking nourishment in the tiny farming community of Narita. The village still seems in a state of shock over the changes brought by the new international airport. Villagers speak little English and we find humor in their attempts to appease the flock of foreigners who've descended on them. Our favorite eatery is closed on this particular day, however, and the owner, not knowing the correct English has hung a sign on his doorknob declaring, "No Today," so we dine elsewhere.

Taiwan, with its teeming markets, Korea, and its stomach-churning kimchee, and the towering high rises of Hong Kong held my fascination for more than a year. Now, however, I longed for Western culture, for someplace where, even if I couldn't speak the language, I could at least read the signs. After all, my heritage is European; my grandfathers emigrated from Italy in the early years of the 20th Century. Europe is where I feel an affinity with the locals. Now, in the irony of all ironies, my company purchased the assets of the bankrupt Pan American World Airways, making us America's largest international air carrier to Europe. In a rather convoluted way, my youthful dream of flying for Pan Am had come true.

THE NORTH SEA, TIME REMAINING, 1:08

Where the spirit does not work with the hand, there is no art. --
-----Leonardo da Vinci

The English coastline is behind us now and ahead of us are the low countries of Holland and Belgium. I idly wonder if Europe is ahead of us, or are we now over it? Is England part of Europe? They are an island to themselves, and yet part of the European Economic Community. I don't know, nor do I know if it matters. What matters at the moment is that the flight attendants must be informed we are one hour from landing. They must stow the galley equipment safely away, complete documents, brush their teeth, and perhaps spray on a little perfume.

The controllers below have cleared us to Frankfurt Airport via Amsterdam, Düsseldorf, and Cologne. Their English is American English, not the King's English, a residue of WWII, I suppose.

The morning makes its appearance in my windshield, and I must once again, as I did nine hours ago, position the plastic sunscreen to reduce the glare. I also stick a small post-it note right where the sun shines through the screen. While the federal authorities frown on this, it actually provides better visibility directly ahead by blocking the glare of the sun. I learned this trick from WWII ace Pappy Boyington, who wrote about it in his book, "Black Sheep Squadron." However, he didn't have post-it notes, so he would use his thumb to blot out the sun, allowing him to spot the enemy who always attacked from that direction.

At this time, we each take a moment to visit the forward "head" as the distraction of personal need can influence one's decision making.

Keyes passes a scrap of paper to me with the latest Frankfurt weather. Visibility is three-fourths of a mile with haze and smoke, and the wind is calm. The Germans burn a lot of wood for heat in the winter, and undoubtedly give no thought to its effect on our landing. Moreover, we will land facing the morning sun—its glare further reducing forward visibility. It doesn't matter whether we can or cannot see the runway. Using our aircraft's automatic landing capabilities combined with special runway lighting and markings, we need not see anything until we are on the ground; and then special runway turnoff lights will guide us clear of the runway. It rarely works this way, though. Not just because the weather rarely is that poor, but because it usurps the very skills attained through years of training and experience. After all, piloting an aircraft to a successful landing in any weather is the epitome of all that an airline pilot knows. And what if the autopilot fails and the airline pilot has not maintained the skill he now needs more than ever? Would you trust your surgeon to operate when his experience consists only of prescribing pills?

All humans, in order to maintain their skills, must practice. A machine will perform consistently without practice. It will, however, inevitably fail and it must be tested regularly—and there is the rub. In one month an international pilot typically makes four round trips from North America to Europe, meaning he gets a total of eight landings. If the first officer makes half of these, then the captain only makes four landings a month. An aircraft theoretically can make 15 round trips a month. Regulations demand that at least once every 30 days pilots use the automatic system for landing, regardless of landing conditions, just to prove the system functions. All told, that means each month a pilot loses one-fourth of his landing practice. That is why today I will manually fly the approach to Frankfurt Airport.

We cross the German border, and I can see Düsseldorf, ahead and below. I remember a time early in my airline career when I crewed with Jack Lewis, a B-17 bomber pilot during the "Good War." His aerial view of Germany probably didn't differ much from my view now, only his payload consisted of bombs, and not passengers. He talked lovingly of the B-17 as the "Queen of the Skies," but never spoke of actually dropping the bombs. I miss him.

Glancing at the flight plan, I see we are approaching our "TOD" or top-of-descent. Bringing a modern airliner to earth involves a complex set of calculations. Viewed from the ground, the most economical descent would look like a parabolic curve— shallow in the beginning, and steep at the end. This must be balanced, however, with passenger comfort, cabin pressurization, and the whims of air traffic control, the final arbiter.

Gordon makes our desire known to air traffic control, and we are cleared to descend to flight level 240. With my thumb I rotate a small wheel located on the glare shield panel. It controls the autopilot in pitch, and my action causes the nose of our aircraft to pitch slightly down. We begin our descent. At the same time, I reduce engine power slightly, allowing gravity to increase our velocity, still keeping within a maximum allowable speed. I allow the autopilot to control the aircraft until we reach 10,000 feet altitude, at which time I disconnect the autopilot, and take control of the aircraft manually. My excuse in doing this is that I am keeping my skills polished. The truth, of course, is this is the part of flying I love the most.

There is a switch labeled "seat belt" above my head on the overhead control panel. When pushed it illuminates the word "on." This also informs the flight attendants we are about 25 minutes from touchdown, allowing them time to secure the cabin and check on each passenger.

Keyes has been listening to the "ATIS" or Automatic Terminal Information Service at Frankfurt Airport. A continuous broadcast tells us the current weather, type of instrument approach, and runway in use. If any aid to navigation is "not in service" or there is construction near the runway, we will learn of it now. Avoiding surprise is essential to a safe landing.

Air traffic control has cleared us to FL 80; this is about 8,000 feet above sea level but not exactly. For our altimeter (which is nothing more than an air pressure barometer) to read the exact altitude above sea level a correction must be obtained from the airport of intended landing. Keyes has gotten this information from ATIS. When we land in Frankfurt our altimeter will read 364 feet as this is the actual altitude of Frankfurt airport above sea level. Many years ago British Airlines set their altimeters to read zero altitude on landing. If one forgot to set the altimeter properly before landing, one could find that he had flown "six feet under" sea level, so to speak.

Today all modern jet aircraft sport "radar altimeters" that show the actual altitude above the terrain as you approach the runway. They are electronic and not subject to the fickleness of Mother Nature.

Descending to 10,000 feet, I begin to slow the TriStar from our descent speed of 500 knots; most of the civilized world has a 250-knot speed restriction below this altitude. Believe it or not, you can get a ticket for exceeding the speed limit. The penalty for this violation is not merely monetary, but can result in the loss of one's flying license and consequently, livelihood. It is not a time for carelessness: all idle conversation is put on hold until we are safely on the ground.

With control of the aircraft in my hands, we continue our descent at the legal speed. I call for the approach checklist, and Keyes begins calling out the items while Gordon and I respond appropriately. It feels good to actually have the control wheel in

226

my hands. For the past ten hours, I have pushed buttons and turned knobs to control the aircraft. I did this not out of laziness, but because the autopilot can control the aircraft in a manner far more precisely than can be managed by a human pilot, thereby saving time and fuel. Now it is time for me to exercise the skills acquired in my more than thirty-five years of flight. My pilot logbook shows more than 24,000 flying hours—almost two years and seven months aloft. It has been said God does not count the hours spent in flight toward one's allotted time on earth. I hope it is true!

We now are in contact with Frankfurt approach control. Using their radar they will ask us to fly a heading to intercept the approach course about five miles from the end of the runway. They also issue a clearance allowing us to execute an ILS (instrument landing system) approach to runway 7 left when our navigation instruments receive the final approach course signal. From this point until we land safely, air traffic control monitors our progress, but control of the aircraft rest entirely in our hands.

I cannot see the runway as ground visibility is about three-fourths of a mile, but it is much worse from our cockpit as the glare of the sun diffuses in the haze and smoke, reducing forward visibility to almost nothing. Gordon monitors my actions while keeping an eye outside. That is what he is supposed to do. This allows me to concentrate fully on flying the airplane, and intercepting the ILS course. Keyes ensures that all checklist items have been completed, and communicates with the flight attendants to assure all is secure in the passenger cabin.

Two yellow needles on my flight director (the primary flight instrument) concern me at this time. One is horizontal, indicating the safe descent path, and the other is vertical, representing the runway centerline. We are 2,500 feet above the runway with the airport to our left. I watch the horizontal bar move down the face of the instrument, and when it centers, I will begin a descent. Simultaneously, the vertical bar begins to move from the right side of the flight instrument, and I will begin a left turn toward the airport, keeping it centered in a perfect cross with the horizontal bar. As we slow the aircraft we must extend the wing flaps to maintain control at low speed. At 170 knots, the controls on the TriStar are smooth and light, not much different than the power steering on your car when you are parallel parking. My left hand is on the control wheel and my right hand grips the throttle much as I did ten hours ago at takeoff. The difference now, of course, is that gravity is bringing our airplane down, and I only have to make small movements of the throttle to produce large changes in speed. I call out "gear down" and Gordon moves the gear handle to the down position while Keyes checks for three green lights, indicating all three landing gears are down and safely locked. At about five miles from the runway end I ask for landing flaps and "before landing checklist." Keyes reads and Gordon responds.

Gordon contacts Frankfurt tower, and we are cleared to land. The cockpit is eerily quiet, except for the whine of the Rolls Royce turbofan engines. Now I am in my element, and I can assure you that every line pilot who ever occupied the left seat feels exactly the same way. My ego overwhelms me. I will slick this on so they will not realize they are on the ground. For every pilot understands that only a smooth landing will make a perfect flight. Only a grease job will bring praise. Perhaps a mediocre landing might be excused, but a hard one is intolerable. A poor landing is like a moustache on the Mona Lisa, a fly in your soup. It cannot be salvaged, only borne with disappointment.

Our airspeed is now 130 knots, about 30 percent above aerodynamic stall speed. To maintain this speed I manipulate the center engine in small increments using all three only when a larger speed correction is necessary.

All pilots know that if there is a "secret" to a good landing it is a stable and well-trimmed approach. This requires steady airspeed, a smooth descent path—neither too high nor too low—and the use of trim controls to remove any control pressures. If you've got all these in place, then even if you removed your hands from the controls, the aircraft would continue to the ground in the proper landing attitude. Only then can one exercise the finesse needed those last few inches to "grease it on."

At the moment, I have achieved this stable "state of grace." The runway rapidly nears but for now it matters not if I can see it. I scan the flight instruments, leaving my eyes on any one for only an instant: airspeed indicator, altimeter, vertical speed indicator, and the primary flight instrument—the flight director. I now include one other instrument in this scan: the radar altimeter. I've set it for 100 feet above the ground, our minimum descent altitude. If I do not see the runway touchdown zone at 100 feet, we must abandon the approach. There is little room for error.

Gordon calls out "200 feet above minimums" indicating that we are two hundred feet from being 100 feet above the airport. Almost immediately after that, he calls out "100 feet above minimums, runway in sight." I steal a quick glance out the windshield, not wanting to fully abandon my instruments until I, too, see the runway. At last I make visual contact with a sea of white lights, and then the green centerline lights, and I mentally revert to visual flight.

As we cross the approach end of the runway I smoothly squeeze off the throttles with my right hand while at the same time using my left thumb to roll in a little pitch trim to reduce the control-wheel backpressure. Now the fun begins. At this point a good landing can become mediocre or worse. It is not just a function of depth perception, although that certainly is an important element. Now is where the term "flying by the seat of your pants" gains real meaning, for it is the ability to sense the motion of the aircraft at this critical point that is all the difference.

With the throttles fully closed, I level the aircraft just above the runway. I do not know how many feet that is but perhaps one or two. As our airspeed decreases I sense the aircraft wanting to settle on the runway ... no, not yet ... it is too soon to land so I raise the nose of the TriStar just a little bit. Now I can feel the ground effect cushioning our descent just as it does for a pelican soaring above an ocean wave. Again I feel the aircraft settle, and I ease the nose ever so slightly higher and wait for the rumble signaling that our tires have met the runway. It is not over yet. As the tires kiss the runway, they begin to rotate creating a mild vibration felt through my seat, and from the control wheel. If I relax at this point, the aircraft will plop to the ground as the landing struts suddenly compress, thus turning a good landing into a mediocre one. So, I maintain control-wheel back- pressure, keeping the nose of the aircraft high until I feel the automatic wing spoilers deploy and the entire TriStar settle upon its wheeled legs. Now I fly the nose of the aircraft to the ground, trying to land the nose wheel with the same gracefulness granted our main gear. Holding forward pressure on the control wheel I gently apply the brakes while at the same time bringing the reverse levers up to idle reverse thrust. Keyes verifies that all three engines are in reverse, and I increase thrust while increasing the pressure on the wheel brakes. Glancing down the runway, I pick out the turnoff I know I can make without undue braking, adjusting braking and reversing so as to arrive at the turnoff at a safe speed. Smoothness is the order of the day; no jackrabbit stops are tolerated. I liken this to a high-speed train entering the station and stopping the first class car right in front of the waiting passengers.

As we clear the runway, Gordon is busy retracting flaps, communicating with Frankfurt ground control, and switching off un-needed systems.

"Nice landing, Captain." A compliment from Keyes, the pilot on board who knows the good from the bad more than any of us, and it warms my heart.

Not all landings go as well as this one. Fickle wind, short runways, poor weather conditions and pilot fatigue can all serve to spoil one's moment of glory; but on this February day in 1994 we would not be denied.

1995

I know of no other skill, craft, profession or endeavor that is outlawed at age 60 except that of Airline Pilot. ----*Anonymous*

With the purchase and integration of the remains of Pan American Airways, my company presented me with a world greatly expanded from the one I had signed on to fly in so many years ago. Not in my wildest dreams as a boy did I imagine I would one day execute the difficult approach to Hong Kong's Kai Tak airport, or find myself converting feet into meters, as required by the air traffic controllers of Russia's St. Petersburg airport. In Hong Kong, I gained a new appreciation for the term "personal space." In St. Petersburg, I grew to appreciate my incredible good fortune as I observed an airport littered with the abandoned hulks of the communist civil aviation industry, and a dingy city in desperate need of paint and restoration.

As it offered a wider choice of flight destinations, I changed my base of flying to Atlanta, where I could choose flights between London, Paris, Nice, Munich, Stuttgart, Dublin, Rome, Barcelona, Madrid, Hamburg, Vienna, Prague, Zurich, and, of course, Frankfurt and St. Petersburg. Most of the flights from Atlanta took three days to complete. This consisted of a round trip from Atlanta to one or two European cities. Occasionally, however, I would choose to fly the longer six and even twelve-day trips, as I was still living in Dallas, which required me to commute to Atlanta to begin my journey. Four roundtrips to Europe in 12 days were normal. U.S. and foreign immigrations officials recognized the futility of stamping our passports each time we landed, therefore, those wanting a "souvenir stamp" had to ask.

It is often said of any voyage that getting there is half the fun. Whether one speaks of air travel, or the voyage of life, I have found this to be so. Perhaps it is a weakness in my character that having found success in an endeavor my fascination wanes, and I search out a new experience, one that will involve me in body and spirit. When I arise from sleep each morning, I cannot tolerate the thought of facing a day exactly like the one before. There is so much in life to experience, how can one possibly fit it in during the brief time allotted to us on this earth? I'd like to think that in a previous life I might have been an eagle, but others have said no, just a curious cat. Perhaps they are right.

It is inevitable then, that my desire to visit greater numbers of foreign cities would begin to wane. The toll on my health from the ubiquitous time zone changes began to show. Flight crews are also victims of jet lag. I considered transferring to domestic flying but that would require being away from home more days each month than required in the international division. And, of course, there is the matter of money. As I approached the mandatory retirement age of 60, I found I had not prepared my finances as astutely as I might have. A reduction in salary didn't figure positively in my financial planning. Other factors worked to cool my passion for flying the line, not the least of which is a changed attitude toward my profession shown by the public and the government. The public thought we were under-worked and overpaid, while the Federal Aviation Administration thought we were careless, and clueless. When a U.S. air carrier suffered an accident, the press promptly trumpeted that the FAA is not doing its job policing the airlines. Ultimately, the line pilot suffered from this increased policing.

A captain flying for a U.S. air carrier must receive a physical examination every six months to maintain a valid pilot license. He also must be checked for flying proficiency twice a year utilizing a simulator, and once a year while flying the line. Additionally, every pilot in line service must attend recurrent ground school on the aircraft he is currently operating. Failure to pass the above tests, courses, and examinations can result in the suspension of his pilot license. A line pilot also must attend courses yearly on such topics as anti-hijacking, carrying dangerous goods, and crew resource management. I know of no other profession in the entire world that requires this degree of testing, training, and oversight. I tell you this not because it is a bad thing; it isn't, and it is more than necessary. It does, however, provide ample opportunity to those few individuals with small minds and petty personalities, who exist in every government bureaucracy, to create a "hell on earth" for the unlucky line pilot whose fate it is to fall under their jurisdiction.

In 1995, the entire airline industry struggled financially from the after-effect of the Gulf War. My company's integration of the Pan Am European operations had proved costly and complex. A surplus of pilots developed as flying was curtailed to meet waning passenger demand. Rumors of a company sponsored "early retirement package" became the topic of conversation in crew lounges system wide. The idea appealed to me as I had concluded that the best was already behind me, and perhaps it was time to call it a career. Recalling once again the theory from the late aviation writer E. K. Gann, who wrote that the best age for an airline pilot is about 35, I realized this was no longer true. Gann correctly understood in his era the necessity for the motor skills of youth, the physical characteristics and aggressiveness that peak at that age. Today, however, airline flying requires a different set of skills, and a less aggressive approach to flying the aircraft, as electronics and computers automate tasks that once required more basic stick and rudder techniques. The old "lone eagle" fighter pilot mentality has been abandoned and CRM is the new buzzword. New skills are being taught to enable crews to deal with the increasing problems associated with the greater passenger capacity of modern "wide body" jet aircraft. All of these factors weighed heavily on my mind as I struggled with the decision whether or not to retire.

In May 1995, in command of a flight from Munich, Germany to New York's JFK I watched as my first officer, a young woman, smoothly manipulated the controls toward our landing. Unusual as it may seem, this was my first experience with a female first officer, although on many occasions in the past I had second officers of the opposite sex. As I watched her fly the aircraft with expertness and proficiency, I realized she represented the new generation, and I began to feel my age. Perhaps it was time to let it go.

A short time after returning home, a medical condition temporarily kept me grounded. After counting the time to recovery, and the time to my 60th birthday, I knew I had commanded my last flight as an airline pilot.

EPILOGUE

On September 11, 2001 while writing the chapter "Electric Jet," I watched in horror along with hundreds of millions of others, as 19 evil men attacked the United States of America. They chose as their weapons the very aircraft I was writing about, the Boeing 757 and 767 transport aircraft. Fully understanding the genius wrought by the Boeing engineers, these misfits of Islam used that creation in a diabolical display of inhumanity.

When the Boeing Aircraft Company hit upon the idea to build two completely different aircraft with identical cockpits, it did so with the notion it would save lives, not end them. It did so for reasons of efficiency and safety, not heinousness and depravity.

The terrorists' intent was to inflict massive loss of life, the kind one would expect from a nuclear explosion or natural disaster. They were successful, but they also accomplished something no natural disaster ever could. They changed the world's air transportation system forever.

For seventy-five years the aviation industry has fought the evil gods of fear. In minutes, 19 miserable miscreants rescued them from banishment.

The world's airlines will adapt to this new reality. No longer will crews be taught in silly hi- jacking ground schools to use cooperation with terrorists on board, so as not to alarm the passengers. And no longer will passengers stand idly by as evil marches them toward certain death. And finally there is a great debate about allowing the airline pilot to carry a fire-arm.

Those against allowing guns in the cockpit feel they will go off "willy nilly," that only people trained in the proper use of fire arms can be trusted with them. Well, let me say that a handgun is the ultimate point and shoot device. It does not take any more training than what you get from a good western movie. In no more than ten minutes anyone can learn to fire a handgun. What is required, however, is that the person in charge of the handgun be a responsible, educated and mentally stable individual who is constantly scrutinized and tested on frequent occasions and who maintains a record of stability over a long period of time. This sure does sound like the Captain of an airliner to me. After all, isn't this the same person that all passengers trust with their life every time they board an airplane?

The chaos that is the airline industry in 2002 will one day return to normal. The trouble is, what is normal for the airline industry is chaos to all others. The president of Continental Airlines said, "This is a stupid industry run by stupid people." I think what he was trying to say is that the airline industry has always been populated with dreamers and adventurers. The industry as a whole never really subscribed to the capitalist free market system that American industry thrives on. It is an industry that never really cared if there were profits, just so long as they could offer the newest and fastest aircraft serving the most glamorous destinations and still stay in business. In the words of Leonardo da Vinci: *"When once you have tasted flight, you will forever walk the earth with your eyes turned skyward, for there you have been, and there you will always long to return."*

During most of the 35 years I worked in the airline industry there was a presumption that supersonic air travel was right around the corner. While it is available to the very wealthy, I am disappointed the economics have not evolved so that all people could share in this advanced technology. From Lindbergh in 1927 to Samuel Miller, in 1958, aircraft speed increased from 110 mph to 600 mph. Since 1958 we have added not a single mile per hour to the speed of the jet transport. This will change someday, and I envy those who will be sitting at the controls of those sub-orbital transports.

As for me, I can only quote my fellow aviator Jack Keyes when he said: *"If my life as an airline pilot were a video, I would hit the rewind button and do it all over again."*

William L. Ippolito
Sept 10, 2002

Email
williamippolito@cs.com

GLOSSARY

DME
Distance Measuring Equipment utilizes UHF radio frequencies to indicate line of sight distance from the ground transmitter to the aircraft receiver.

FEATHER THE PROPELLER
In the event of engine failure on propeller driven aircraft, it is necessary to bring the propeller blades in line with the air stream so the engine cannot "wind mill." A wind-milling propeller creates so much drag and loss of aircraft performance that the good engine or engines may not be able to compensate. Therefore loss of aircraft control is eminent.

FLIGHT DIRECTOR
The Flight Director is the primary flight instrument when the aircraft is under manual control. Two thin bars displayed on a small TV type screen, (in older aircraft a round instrument) one vertical and the other horizontal, form a symmetrical cross when the aircraft is positioned correctly. The vertical bar indicates left or right of course while the horizontal bar indicates high or low of desired path.

FLIGHT LEVEL
An altitude above sea level read from a barometric altimeter that is set to a standard pressure of 29.92 inches of mercury.

ILS
Instrument Landing System utilizes two VHF radio beams, one for left-right and one for up-down, to create a safe approach and

descent path; this path can be received by any aircraft equipped with the proper instrumentation and radio receiver.

INS
Inertial Navigation System uses spinning gyros and a computer to calculate the motion of the aircraft relative to the ever spinning earth. Sensitive measuring devices can tell "where its at" by knowing where its supposed to be. A computer calculates the difference between "where it isn't" and "where it is" and creates a course correction to where it is supposed to be.

IFR
Instrument Flight Rules are the rules and procedures one must follow to fly in clouds where it is impossible to see other aircraft or even the ground. Separation of aircraft in flight is under the control of ground based Air Traffic Control. Airline aircraft always operate under IFR procedures even when the weather is clear.

KNOTS
Derived from the ancient maritime system of measuring speed by throwing a knotted line overboard and counting how many knots pass through your hand in a given time. In contemporary use it means "nautical miles per hour."

NAUTICAL MILE
One nautical mile is 6,076.1 feet in length. It is also equal in distance to one "minute" of the earth's latitude. One degree of the earth's latitude contains "sixty minutes" and is therefore sixty nautical miles in width.

STATUTE MILE
A statute mile is 5,280 feet in length. It is used generally only in the USA to measure ground distance and speed in automobiles.

VFR
Visual Flight Rules are the rules and procedures one follows when the weather is clear and separation of aircraft in flight is accomplished by the "see and be seen" method. Airline aircraft in scheduled service never operate under these rules.

VOR
Very high frequency Omni Range is a modern radio navigation system allowing multiple navigation courses between radio stations.

WAYPOINT
A point in space used for navigation. A waypoint can be a radio facility or just a point delineated by latitude and longitude.